RACING A SPORTS CAR

The Author and Mrs. Mortimer

RACING
A SPORTS CAR

by

CHARLES MORTIMER

1951

LONDON

G. T. FOULIS & CO., LTD.

7 Milford Lane, Strand, W.C.2

Printed in Great Britain by
THE MARSHALL PRESS LIMITED
7, Milford Lane, Strand, London, W.C.2.

FOREWORD

By His Grace The Duke of Richmond and Gordon

I AM very honoured and delighted to write a foreword to this little book, and it has been most interesting reading the proof pages.

Motor-racing is now on the up-grade all the time in this country, and in my capacity as President of the B.A.R.C. and the promoter of the Goodwood Circuit, I am continually being consulted by prospective owner drivers with the urge to " have a go."

Very few young men can find either the money or the time to enter the game with a full-blown ex-Grand Prix formula machine and all the ramifications that involves, but quite a number come to me toying with the idea of making a start in sports car racing. Exactly what this involves is very ably set out in this story of a season's racing with a Silverstone Healey.

Charles Mortimer is, of course, an experienced driver, having graduated through that hard and invaluable school of motor-bike racing, but this should in no way depress the would-be novice, for Mrs. Charles (Jean) Mortimer was as inexperienced at the beginning of the season as she was subsequently successful in her debut.

The story of her introduction to the game as a driver is in itself a lesson to the newcomer, and probably as valuable as all the wealth of technical and financial tips on other pages.

From practical experience as well as by observation of others, I can testify that discipline and the humble approach are the keynotes of successful apprenticeship to motor-racing. There is no doubt that Jean's superlative efforts in this, her first season, were due to her aptitude for listening, watching others and learning. A perfect pupil, in fact.

Motor-racing is a science and the driving is an art into which there is no short-cut entry, but it is surprising how many newcomers think otherwise. Many a time I have stifled a moan to see an unknown name down as the new driver of some old racer of dubious controllability. Furthermore, quite a few of these old " war horses " still exist and harass the scrutineers.

Far better graduate through the sports car classes and I congratulate Charles Mortimer on having provided just the information required by those who would try their hands.

RICHMOND.

CONTENTS

ILLUSTRATIONS

RACING A SPORTS CAR

CHAPTER I

I Buy a Sports Car

MUCH has been written since the war on the subject of Motor Racing in most of its forms, but far too little, in the opinion of many, has been said on the subject of sports-car racing. It has seemed to me that, with the tremendous growth in popularity of motor racing generally and particularly sports-car racing, there must be a formidable army of sports-car owners who would like to race in sports-car events but who are held back by having no knowledge of the cost in time and money.

Accordingly, therefore, I decided to try to find out these things by buying and racing a sports car of a type that can be bought by anyone, and by planning a programme of racing events such as could reasonably be undertaken by an amateur driver, racing with a view to keeping costs in time and money to a minimum.

The idea originally occurred to me when watching the Production Car Race at the B.R.D.C. Meeting sponsored by the *Daily Express* at Silverstone in August, 1949. The first problem to be solved appeared to be the selection of a suitable car and as it seemed certain that the ultimate choice would come from the ranks of the cars running in that particular event, I made a careful study of each entry during the practice period before that race.

I came away from the meeting with no firm decision taken in this direction but feeling more sure than ever that there was, in fact, tremendous interest in this particular form of motor racing. Having thought over things carefully it seemed to me that there were certain obvious points to aim for in choosing a suitable car. Amongst these were low or, at any rate, medium basic price, easily obtainable spares, an enthusiastic works and, if possible, a car having a largish unblown engine requiring a minimum of maintenance.

The final selection was made on reading in the *Autocar* and the *Motor* the preliminary reports of the Silverstone Model Healey, and the thing was irrevocably settled after I had read the excellent road test in *Motor Sport*. My principal aims throughout were to keep the car as far as possible to standard specification and to drive it to the various race meetings under its own steam, thereby cutting out that host of overhead expenses caused by having to use a racing van together with its attendants, and to keep down expenses in every direction to an absolute minimum.

At the beginning of January, 1950, I discovered that, by sheer good fortune, I could, if I wished, become the owner of a Silverstone Healey with a short but quite distinguished history. The car in question was the one that had been driven into fourth place by Tony Rolt in the race that I had watched with such great interest at Silverstone in August, 1949. It was, when offered to me, completely stripped down, and in view of the fact that it was available immediately I was delighted to acquire it without further delay. It was agreed that the car should be built up in exactly the same trim as it had previously run and delivery was promised not later than the end of January, 1950.

At this stage I should, perhaps, explain how I came to purchase this particular car. I had raced motor-cycles and cars fairly regularly at Brooklands before the war and had hoped to be able to run in Formula events when racing began again in 1946. The steadily rising cost of Grand Prix Formula racing and the great difficulty in obtaining a suitable machine of modern design had, however, reduced me once more to the ranks of spectator.

I had almost given up the idea of racing again when my business partner, Alastair Baring, purchased this particular

Silverstone Model Healey shortly after the B.R.D.C. Race in 1949. I was allocated the task of collecting it from the works at Warwick and, in this one run of approximately 90 miles I decided that if I was to race again at all, then it would ultimately have to be on one of these cars.

In December, therefore, I decided to go ahead and acquire one. I told Baring and we discussed the question of close co-operation in running two cars. We both felt, however, that in running identical machines we should to some extent be competing too directly against each other. It was agreed, therefore, that another machine of a different make and capacity should be acquired to be driven by him and that I should take over the Healey from him.

Everything appeared to be working out excellently, although it was apparent that, even with two cars of different type and capacity we should have to discuss and lay out our proposed programmes with great care. This was also necessary from a business angle, for Baring was Chairman and Managing Director of a group of companies in which I also had a small, but active, interest. Also senior to myself in the group was our co-director, Ted Probert, and it would have been obviously unsatisfactory from the point of view of the business itself and from his personal angle for both Baring and myself to have been away together for long periods. But as my intention from the start had been to undertake a season's racing at a cut price, this situation, I thought, should not really arise. I did not want to go far afield for long periods because, apart from any other reasons, I was not well established as a sports-car driver abroad and could not therefore have relied on receiving attractive offers from Continental race organizers.

I decided, therefore, to undertake a programme of races including one main and one minor race meeting per month throughout the season from April to September inclusive, and at the same time to keep my radius of travel as short as possible. I found that the International Calendar and Home Fixture lists were both available from the R.A.C. in early January, and, having studied them, I decided to make the B.A.R.C. dates at Goodwood the basis of my programme. In addition to this I was very keen indeed to achieve acceptance for the R.A.C. T.T. in September, although I did not feel very confident in getting accepted for this race unless the car performed creditably throughout the earlier part of the season.

I should have liked to have entered the car in the 24-Hour Races at Le Mans and Spa, but here again, the two main considerations, cost in time and money, decided me against. In any case, both these races were scheduled to be held quite a bit earlier on in the season than the T.T. and with the greatly over subscribed entry lists for both events I should probably have been unable to achieve acceptance anyway. I felt, however, that I must aim to run the car in at least one main event on the Continent and I decided, therefore, to enter for the long distance event to be held at Montlhéry, near Paris, scheduled to be held on July 23rd.

I wanted to run the car as far as possible in races and not in sprints partly because I personally felt that it was more suitable for this type of competition, but mainly because I preferred races, although it looked as though I might have to fill one or two gaps in the programme with an odd sprint or hill-climb.

As soon as I had bought the car I also acquired a large note-book in which I jotted down any relevant information whatever regarding it. This went with the car wherever it raced and every scrap of information including such items as accessory manufacturers' telephone numbers, Press road tests, a copy of the season's programme, and, of course, notes of any work done to the car together with details of the results were all carefully noted. This item of equipment proved to be of great value time and time again and I would strongly recommend anyone contemplating a racing programme, however limited, to include it.

By the middle of January, therefore, I had drawn up a programme on the following lines:—

April

10th.—Goodwood Easter Meeting.
29th.—Vintage Car Club, Silverstone Meeting.

May

6th.—Goodwood Club Meeting.
27th.—Goodwood Whitsun Meeting.

JUNE
17th.—Goodwood Club Meeting.

JULY
23rd.—Montlhéry (Long Distance) Race.

AUGUST
12th.—Goodwood Club Meeting.
26th.—B.R.D.C. Races, Silverstone.

SEPTEMBER
2nd.—Brighton Speed Trials.
16th.—R.A.C. Tourist Trophy.
30th.—Goodwood Autumn Meeting.

April and May appeared to work out well, although a main event had not yet been selected for June or a minor one for July. I hoped that the B.R.D.C. date in August would include a suitable event in which case that month could be considered planned and September appeared to include, if anything, a surfeit of suitable events. At this stage, therefore, I felt that nothing more could be done towards planning the programme and I turned therefore to making plans for the maintenance of the car.

The Healey was assembled and ready for test on January 17th. No basic alterations whatever had been made but the body had been removed and the engine stripped completely, particular care being taken in reassembly. The only item on which work was done was the cylinder head and, even then, time was only spent in improving the finish of the ports and combustion chambers and not in alteration of port shapes or actual enlargement of them.

The removal of the body enabled the chassis parts to be carefully examined and checked, but it was not anticipated that much work would be necessary in view of the comparative newness of the car. This proved to be the case and practically nothing had to be done, although, here again, everything was very carefully reassembled.

All this work was in progress when I took over the Healey and it was agreed that it should be completed prior to the actual handing over of the car. I should make this point clear because my aim throughout this book has been to give others an idea of the cost of preparing and racing a car, and in this case I obviously reaped the benefit of work that had been put into the car before it reached my hands.

Nevertheless, I would not presume to suggest that such careful preparation is essential for short events at home or even, possibly, for events of up to one hour's duration. For longer events one cannot pay too much attention to detail and it is amazing how apparently well-mounted components will work loose and disappear during a long race.

On January 17th, therefore, I took delivery of the car, having given it a short test on the road, accompanied by Baring's racing mechanic, Buckle, who had been responsible for carrying out the work I have described. I feel that considerable credit was due to him, for not one snag cropped up during that first run. The engine started at the first touch of the button, was warmed up and had the tappets adjusted before going out on the road. We then went for a test run of about twenty miles during which the car appeared to have all the speed and perhaps more than it had had prior to being stripped down, while it was also equally smooth running and in every way as good, or better, than before the work had been undertaken.

For me, the situation was quite unparalleled because, for the first time in my life, I found myself ready to go motor racing little more than half-way through January.

In previous years, I recollected, I had still been frantically chasing round in March for bits and pieces for the obsolete Formula 1 machine that I had then been running. As I drove the Healey home after having taken delivery, I could hardly believe that, for the first time ever, I was ready three months in advance!

I should explain that the car was in absolutely standard form, running on Pool petrol with a compression ratio of 6.9 to 1, and I intended to keep it in this form until I was compelled to alter it, either in order to obtain more speed or, if alterations were necessitated, in order to comply with the regulations for any specific event.

The Healey was cellulosed red when I took delivery and I knew that sooner or later I should have to have it painted

[Photos : Guy Griffiths

*" I resolved to do my utmost to stick as closely as
possible to McAlpine "*

GOODWOOD, MAY, 1950

*" . . . I was not keen to pass him, even if I could,
during the second lap "*

GOODWOOD, MAY, 1950

*" Another hundredth of a second would have given us
fastest Sports Car time "*

WEST ESSEX CAR CLUB, CHELMSFORD SPEED TRAILS, MARCH, 1950

C

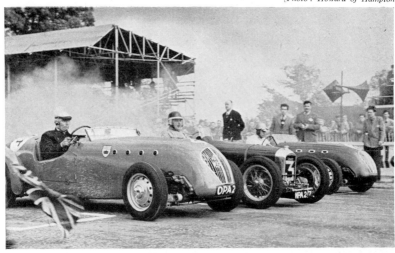

"At the fall of the flag"
GOODWOOD WHITSUN MEETING, 1950

" Ourselves fourth and Onslow Bartlett fifth"
BLANDFORD, WHIT MONDAY, 1950

20

British Racing Green, probably the first time I competed abroad. Although I was looking forward to running the car in a Continental race I regretted the necessity of having to repaint it, partly on the grounds of expense and partly because I liked it better red.

My sole expense so far had been the actual purchase price of the car and I now had to start thinking carefully of ways and means of keeping running expenses down. In the few post-war events in which I had competed with old Formula 1 cars I had had such a surfeit of assistants and general hangers on with their various hotel bills and numerous expenses that, at first, I could hardly visualize racing without them.

I began by wondering whether I should need one attendant or two. I felt sure I could certainly get away with it without two, and ended by eliminating permanent attendants altogether. Obviously, I should require someone with experience and energy in attendance at my pit at long races, but until then I felt sure I could make the thing work by enlisting the aid of enthusiastic friends and relations.

In all my various ventures my number one supporter has been my wonderful wife, Jean, and I knew that I could always rely on her whole-hearted support. We talked the thing over and agreed between us that, as far as possible, we would endeavour to run the car with the minimum amount of outside help and that, in order that the affair should not become one sided, we would share the driving as well, Jean driving when there were ladies' classes and I elsewhere. We had just decided this when the West Essex Car Club announced that they were running a Sprint Meeting at Chelmsford on March 26th. The event was to take place on an airfield and was to be run over a dead straight standing start kilometre, and as there was an award to be won for the best time achieved by a lady driver, Jean was obviously entitled to first crack. Accordingly, we put in an entry which was accepted and in due course we set out on March 26th, in the Healey, full of hope and enthusiasm. We left home at Weybridge at 8 a.m. after making arrangements for the care of our eleven-month-old son, also an enthusiastic motorist, by the way, and after a cold run down to Chelmsford we arrived at Boreham Hill airfield at around 11 a.m.

The course proved to be slightly uphill with a good surface, very wide and with a good pull up at the finish, the competitors running in pairs and returning to the start via a perimeter road. There was a large entry of varying quality and by midday there was a crowd of spectators numbering several thousand. To enthusiasts like ourselves, the first meeting of the season, whether it be large or small, has always a very special attraction. New cars appear and many of the cars running in previous seasons have changed hands and the variety of reds, blues, greens and many other colours combine to make a really vivid picture and this, together with the sound of the highly tuned engines, gives one a real uplift after the long winter months. At this particular meeting, we were interested to see Anthony Crook competing in an unfamiliar supercharged Alta, while G. E. Matthews was running two 3½-litre Jaguars, one in the over 3-litre sports class and the other, a very famous machine which used to be driven at one time by Mrs. Wisdom, in the corresponding racing class. Oscar Moore was there with his well-known O.B.M., a vehicle which began life as a 328 Frazer-Nash B.M.W., and we were very intrigued to find that another Healey " Silverstone " was running. This car was to be driven by L. C. Le Fever and was not directly in competition with us since its entrant had put it in for a class in which there were no fuel restrictions and it was not, therefore, compelled as we were, to run on Pool petrol. In addition, all the wings and even the spare wheel had been removed and as we, in our class, were restricted to running on Pool with full touring equipment including lamps, wings, hood and self-starter, we were watching Le Fever's performance with special interest.

By the time we had strolled up the course and arrived back at the start the smaller capacity sports cars had completed their runs and before long we were waiting on the line with the Healey. The start signals were the usual " 3," " 2," " 1 " and a green light, the numbers lighting up at one second intervals followed by the Green start light at the same interval. We were down to run with F. A. Spiller's supercharged M.G., and as the Green light lit up, both cars made an excellent start and for the first hundred yards there appeared to be little between them. When my wife returned to the paddock she told me that she had finished well ahead of Spiller, and by this time I had been able to procure her time—35.17 secs. I personally was well satisfied with this, but Jean, meanwhile, had discovered that Matthews' time of 34.16 on the 3½-litre Jaguar represented fastest standard sports-car time.

Nothing I could say would convince her that, as we were giving away a litre in engine capacity, for the Healey is 2,443-c.c. and the Jaguar 3,486-c.c., we stood little chance of beating this time on our second run. She was determined to try and, as events proved, she was very nearly successful for, on his second run, Matthews was very slightly slower, clocking 34.20 secs., while my wife improved her time by over a second, managing 34.16 secs., and exactly equalling Matthews' first run time.

Another hundredth of a second would have given us fastest standard sports-car time although, by virtue of the Club's ruling that only one award could be won per entrant, we should not in point of fact have profited. In the official results we were credited with fastest time for a car driven by a lady, although we had, in fact, tied for fastest sports-car time outright with Matthews and won the up to 3-litre standard sports-car class as well. In point of fact, Spiller, who had run with my wife and whose best run was 38.8 secs., was awarded the up to 3-litre class while Matthews—to round off a highly successful day—put up fastest time of day, 29.15 secs. with his other car in the Racing Car Class.

At first sight this method of allocating awards may seem strange, although I personally consider it very fair and even generous on the part of the organizing club. It puts more people on the awards list and prevents one competitor winning a number of other classes besides his own.

Second fastest time of day was put up by Anthony Crook in the Alta in 29.41 secs., although a catastrophe occurred in the engine of this car on its second run. Somewhat to our surprise, Le Fever's time on the other Healey " Silverstone " —35.28 secs.—was not as good as our own, his class being won by Crook in 30.34 secs.

Our first meeting with the car was over and we had achieved some measure of success. We were delighted with the car which had not given us one moment's trouble either on the run down, during the event, or on the way home. On arrival home we reviewed the financial position for the first three months of the year and found that it stood as follows:—The car had cost us the retail figure of £1,246 11s. 8d. and we had, of course, competed with it at one meeting. In addition, we had put in entries for two more, the Goodwood Easter Monday Meeting on April 10th, in which I was to drive in a short handicap race and the first B.A.R.C. Goodwood Club Meeting of the season on May 6th. Ladies were eligible to drive at the latter and so we entered the car in the only two races open to it; a three-lap handicap with Jean as driver and a three-lap scratch race for unblown cars up to 3 litres to be driven by myself.

At the Easter Meeting, as the car was running as a racing car, we were not permitted to carry a spare wheel and as the removal of this item leaves a large gap in the tail of the Healey "Silverstone" we had a panel made up to fit this. We also had to fit an additional mirror and a fire extinguisher in order to conform to the Regulations as laid down by the B.A.R.C. The latter item we did not have to buy as we have always kept an extinguisher as part of our garage equipment. The cost to the end of March, 1950, therefore, was as follows:—

	£	s.	d.
Purchase price of car	1,246	11	8
Tax	10	0	0
Insurance	11	12	3
R.A.C. Competition Licences (two drivers)	2	0	0
West Essex Car Club entries (including membership of the Club)	2	11	6
Fuel used for Chelmsford Speed Trials	0	8	9
One Alloy panel for spare wheel well	2	0	0
Two Mirrors	2	0	0
B.A.R.C. Easter Monday entry (including membership of the Club)	4	13	6
B.A.R.C. Club Meeting entry fees (including membership of the Club)	6	6	0
TOTAL	£1,288	3	8

The insurance cover granted related to road use only. We took out no special cover either for the driver or for the car while it was being raced, beyond the usual third-party cover, the premium for this being usually included in the entry fees for each event. We had also laid in a stock of spares for the car amounting to about £30 worth, but I have not included these in our expense sheet to date because they were being held purely for the sake of convenience and were not intended for immediate use.

The cost therefore for the first three months amounted to £41 12s., excluding the purchase price of the car. We had already had a great deal of fun, and time alone would reveal what it was going to cost us in the future or what results we might achieve as result of our efforts.

CHAPTER II

First Time Out

FOLLOWING quickly on the heels of our Speed Trials at Chelmsford, on March 26th, was the B.A.R.C. Easter Meeting at Goodwood, on April 10th. The Healey was entered for one five-lap handicap in which I was to drive, and on Saturday, April 8th, therefore, we made our way down to Goodwood for the official practising.

On the way down we noticed a slight misfire in the engine which appeared to be caused by fuel starvation. We checked the fuel level and found that the tank was well over half full, and on changing over from the main to the reserve pump the trouble appeared to be cured. We decided, therefore, to practise on the reserve pump and, if we had time, to change the main pump after having put in the necessary number of qualifying laps.

The B.A.R.C. had procured a magnificent entry for their Easter Meeting, including such well-known names as Baron de Graffenried, Reg Parnell and Prince Bira, all of whom were driving the latest 4 CLT. Maserati Grand Prix cars. Other interesting entries were John Heath's beautifully turned out team of 2-litre unsupercharged H.W.M.s These were to be driven by John himself, George Abecassis, Stirling Moss and my partner, Alastair Baring. The cars themselves were composite machines built at H. W. Motors, Ltd., a company in which George and John are directors.

Our practice period was to be short lived, however, for I had only just started to open the car up, having three warming-up laps because I had never been round the course before, when fuel starvation again became apparent, this time on the reserve pump. I pulled in and started to investigate the trouble. I disconnected the fuel line at the carburetter end, switched on the electric reserve pump which gave a poor flow of fuel and was apparently pumping some air. I then tried the main pump which was pumping only air. On checking the fuel level in the tank I found that there were still between six and seven gallons of fuel in the tank—quite enough to supply the main pump and more than enough for the reserve. The pumps were situated on top of the fuel tank which was in the tail of the car and they drew the fuel through two internal pipes running from the top to the bottom of the tank, and unless the trouble lay inside the tank, in which case I could do little about it, the only other possible causes of starvation could be an external air leak or a fault in the pumps themselves.

Having satisfied myself that there were no external air leaks, I changed both pumps, tried the car once again and found that the trouble was just as noticeable as ever. By this time the practice period had ended and as I had had not time to take advantage of it I could obviously not run in the race. It was disappointing, but I realized that we had been very lucky to date and I decided to put the car away and enjoy the meeting as a spectator.

I was certainly in good company in having trouble because " Bira " was in the midst of an appalling and apparently incurable bout of steering wobble. Time after time the car came into the paddock after having done single laps, driven alternately by " Bira " and his mechanic with the front wheels wobbling alarmingly, even at touring speeds. The only other Healey running, a single-seater modified to 2 litre, and driven by R. M. Dryden, was also in trouble with a blown cylinder-head gasket, and as I slaved away, stinking of petrol, I watched with a morbid interest the efforts of the unfortunate " Bira " and debated whether it was preferable to spend an enjoyable Easter Saturday dabbling in petrol or surrounded by rivers of oily water as in the case of poor " Curly " Dryden.

By the time I had finished trying to get to the bottom of my own troubles the practice period was over and we limped home with the car, to garage it until after the meeting.

Easter Monday dawned and one glance at the weather told me that I had missed very little. Torrents of rain and half a gale in the paddock made one wonder whether the meeting would be held, but towards midday the rain became more inter-mittent, although the wind increased in fury until the only habitable places were the refreshment tents, each of which appeared to house about a thousand people standing elbow to elbow. Great credit was due to everyone concerned that the meeting was run off without a hitch and with some magnificent racing into the bargain, the principal events being won by " Bira," de Graffenried and Reg Parnell.

I was unable to spend any more time in endeavouring to trace the cause of the trouble with the car, and I arranged with John Heath that his racing staff should collect the car and should locate and cure the trouble. This proved to be inside the tank as we thought and was, in fact, due to faulty soldering of the fuel-feed pipes at the top of the tank, thereby causing the pumps to pump air and not fuel. This was our first setback of the season and involved the removal of the tank as well as the removal and resoldering of the internal fuel-feed pipes. While the car was in John's capable hands it seemed a good idea for it to be given a thorough check over and it was agreed, therefore, that this should be carried out also. The check over revealed a couple of very slightly bent push-rods, indicating that at some time of its life the engine had been taken up over the safe rev limit. Neither Jean nor I were ever able to agree as to who was the culprit, but we both resolved to be more careful in future.

The only Goodwood lap time we had as a basis to work on was my last practice lap of 2 mins. 7 secs., during which our fuel feed trouble persisted, this lap time representing a speed of 68.00 m.p.h.

As the Goodwood Members' Meeting on May 6th was fast approaching we decided to go down to the circuit again on April 22nd, in order to take advantage of the B.A.R.C. " official " practice day. Jean had never driven on a circuit of any sort before and I had no real knowledge of the Goodwood circuit, having only done a few slow practice laps at Easter, and so we arrived there on Saturday the 22nd, realizing that we had a lot to learn in a short time.

Jean went out on the circuit first and came in, having done two laps in 2 mins. 14 secs. and 2 mins. 15 secs. respectively. She reported all O.K. with the car, but said that she felt " quite clueless." There was nothing very fast out on the circuit at the time so I suggested that she should go for quite a long run of ten to fifteen laps in order to gain confidence and some knowledge of the circuit. She went out again, doing a standing lap of 2 mins. 18 secs., followed by flying laps of 2.11, 2.10, 2.10, 2.9, 2.8 1/5, and 2.7 4/5. She then came in again and I took over, achieving 2.15, 2.3, 2.1, and 1.58, during which I found I learnt a lot. In the first place I found that at least one bend that I had formerly imagined to be a third-gear bend could actually be taken full bore in top thereby improving the lap speed, while I had a feeling that the same thing applied to at least one more.

I came in after having done these four laps and as the times were rather better than I had expected, I decided not to do any more for the time being, so that Jean could have another session without the car being chased round for too many laps. On her second session, Jean managed 2.6, 2.7, 2.4, and 2.3, with a standing lap of 2.15, and as we should obviously be getting some more practice on the day of the next event, we decided to do no more for that day. The car was obviously going as well at the end of the day as it had at the beginning and we accordingly made our way home, stopping for an excellent tea at the Spreadeagle at Midhurst *en route*.

We spent the next day giving the car a thorough check over during the course of which we found that our Goodwood lappery had worn the tyres down very considerably. We had been told by several other regular Goodwood drivers that tyre wear was not light on that circuit in common with most other twisty circuits and so we had expected this, and had already laid in a stock of new tyres, some of which we decided to fit before the meeting on May 6th. We also laid by a stock of replacement plugs: we had, up to now, been using the same set that were fitted when we took over the car and it was obviously time we replaced them. Apart from these items, everything else appeared to be in good order and we decided not to make any other alterations before the next meeting.

The B.A.R.C. Members' Meetings suited our plans particularly well because they were " one-day " meetings. By this I mean that official practice took place on the morning of the meeting and not, as with larger events, on the day before the race.

On May 6th, therefore, we set out once again for Goodwood. The weather was far from ideal and we had a wet run down and, once more, a wet and cold practice period. Our times were considerably down on our last practice times, Jean managing 2 mins. 7 secs. and I, 2 mins. 4 secs. There was plenty of competition at this meeting and I should, perhaps, explain that at these sports-car meetings the regulations regarding fuel stipulated that ordinary pump fuel should be used with the addition of up to 50 per cent. benzol added. We could, therefore, had we wished, have raised the compression ratio of the engine considerably above the standard 6.9 ratio that we were using and could have taken advantage of this concession allowing us to use a percentage of benzol. On the other hand, had we done so, we should have had to change the pistons to lower compression for other meetings at which pump fuel only was allowed and, as we felt that this would involve considerable labour and additional expense, we decided to keep the car running on the lower ratio throughout the season although we realized that we should, sometimes, inevitably be giving away some speed.

There were ten races in all at this meeting, each of which was the same distance, i.e., three laps of the 2.4 mile circuit. In the scratch race in which I was to drive, and which was the third race of the day, there were no fewer than three other " Silverstone " model Healeys. Kenneth McAlpine's Connaught, Oscar Moore's O.B.M., Gilbert Tyrer's very beautiful aerodynamic Mille Miglia Frazer-Nash B.M.W., and a number of other cars, all, of course, under 3-litre capacity.

The Connaught had previously won a race on this circuit at over 73 m.p.h., so I held out little hope of being able to compete with McAlpine and I also felt very dubious about being able to make any real impression on either Moore or Tyrer. Practice times revealed McAlpine to be easily the fastest in this race, with Moore and Tyrer next and myself fourth, the other Healeys being close behind.

Starting positions in scratch races at Goodwood are decided by ballot, and as it would obviously be impossible to start a dozen or more cars abreast the field is lined up in rows of four, and in a short race of this sort it is obviously a great help if one is lucky enough to draw a front-row position. In this case I could not have been more fortunate because on arrival on the starting line I found that I had drawn a position in the front row next to McAlpine with Tyrer in the second row, directly behind me. Oscar Moore had, unfortunately, had trouble at the last moment and was a non-starter.

I resolved to do my utmost to stick as closely as possible to McAlpine, but as soon as the flag had fallen I realized that I just could not compete. He was easily first into the gradual bend immediately after the start followed by Tyrer, myself and one of the other Healeys with the rest of the field already stringing out behind.

Realizing that I could do nothing about the Connaught I decided to concentrate on Tyrer and found that, whereas there was very little difference between the speed of his car and mine, his knowledge of the circuit seemed to be even more limited than my own. During the first lap I noticed at least one point at which he seemed to me to be losing time and I resolved to watch carefully during the second lap and to try and pass him during the third and last lap. I was not keen to pass him, even if I could, during the second lap, first because I felt that I should have been better able to size up the correct spot by waiting, and secondly because the speeds of the two cars were so nearly identical that I was not absolutely sure of being able to stay ahead of him for long, assuming that I could get by.

Towards the end of the second lap, McAlpine was holding a comfortable lead of several hundred yards, and I had already chosen the spot at which I was going to try to pass. It was, for the Healey, the fastest bend on the course on the back leg, and on laps one and two I had noticed Tyrer slow very considerably for it. I decided therefore to drop back behind about fifty or sixty yards and to take the bend as fast as I dare in the hope that he would slow again, thereby enabling me to get by on the exit. These tactics worked well and as we came out together, both cars were absolutely neck and neck. The next bend was a fast right hander and as we went down the straight together I began to wonder who had the best brakes because we were obviously both going to need them badly.   Being on the outside, I should obviously not be so well placed, and it was with a feeling of great relief that I saw the profile of the B.M.W. suddenly recede as Tyrer courteously gave way.

After that it was fairly plain sailing and that was how we finished.   McAlpine's winning speed was 72.00 m.p.h., I was 16.2 secs. behind him and Tyrer .02 secs. behind me.   During a conversation I had afterwards with him he told me that he had never seen the circuit until that day and had only been able to do a very few practice laps that morning.   Both he and McAlpine were using considerably higher compression ratios than we were on the Healey and were both using a percentage of benzol.   Against that, however, their engines were both under 2-litres as compared with the Healey capacity of 2½-litres, so it could truthfully be said that circumstances were fairly even.   Anyhow it had been a grand race from my own point of view and it all contributed to give the practice I so badly needed.

Now it was Jean's turn, and I am afraid that the handicappers had not treated her kindly.   McAlpine was now on the scratch mark, Jean was next to him and received five seconds' start from him in three laps.   She, in turn, conceded three seconds' start to Tyrer and no less than one minute five seconds to the limit men, A. H. Ellis and F. J. Ames, both of whom were driving Ballila Fiats.   There were seventeen entries for the race and whatever her chances were against the fourteen drivers to whom she had to concede start it was more than obvious to me, at any rate, that she could not hope to compete against either McAlpine or Tyrer on such terms. Had I been driving myself I would have felt the same and for anyone driving their first race it was an absolutely impossible handicap.

Nevertheless she was keen to run and so we decided to adopt the following tactics.   Tyrer's car, we now knew, was almost identical in performance to our own, although he himself was a driver of considerable experience and skill.   McAlpine was equally good but had a much faster car.   We estimated that McAlpine would pick up his five seconds conceded to our entry either towards the end of the first lap or the beginning of the second. We knew that we could not possibly pass Tyrer, but it was agreed that Jean should endeavour to keep as close to him as she could, for as long as possible. Having driven behind Tyrer for the greater part of my race, I was able to give Jean one piece of information that I thought might be of considerable help to her. This was that his car was fitted with two very excellent " stop " lights in good working order, one mounted on each of the rear wings. By watching these it was possible to see exactly when he put on his brakes and, as our brakes appeared to be quite as good, if not better than his, it was of considerable assistance to anyone following to study his braking points. We also thought that McAlpine might be slightly delayed while endeavouring to pass Tyrer and hoped that if this was so, we might profit.

Once on the line I felt fearfully responsible and impressed on my poor wife again and again the necessity of giving McAlpine ample room to pass, once he had caught her up. I need not have worried, however, for, watching the race with Mike Oliver, who was helping McAlpine at this meeting, I was tremendously relieved to see the trio heave into view in good order at the end of the first lap, Tyrer ahead of Jean and both of them closely followed by the flying Connaught. All three of them were in the process of overtaking slower cars and they still remained in the same order as they disappeared from view, although the Connaught was close on the tail of the Healey with ample room to pass. I managed to get a view of the situation on the far side of the circuit, saw McAlpine pass my wife and saw him also pass Tyrer. When they appeared again at the pits, McAlpine lay sixth, Tyrer seventh, and Jean tenth. During the last lap each of these three cars drew steadily away from the others and at the finish the Connaught was third, the B.M.W. fourth and our Healey fifth.

We were both satisfied with the day because we had both gained some more knowledge of the circuit. Jean's three lap speeds were 2 mins. 10 secs. from a standing start, 2 mins. 5 secs. and 2 mins. 4 secs. for flying laps by my timing, which gave her an average of over 68 m.p.h. for the three laps from a standing start, a performance which I thought was good for anyone driving in their first race on a crowded circuit such as Goodwood.

Very contented with life in general, we packed up our tools and spares, stowed them in the Healey and set off home. The weather had improved by this time and we decided to stop for dinner at the Talbot Hotel, at Ripley, where we enjoyed a really excellent meal and equally good wine.

We talked over the meeting together and decided that this sports-car racing really was the thing. There was no doubt about it, we were getting value for money and we both agreed that, had we realized it previously, we would have forsaken the old Formula 1 cars more speedily in favour of a good sports car. Outside, the poor old Healey sat once again in the pouring rain and we both felt rather guilty as we looked at it through the window, for we had already come to regard it as a friend. " I must go over the whole thing with a hose and a grease gun, to-morrow," I said. " Good idea," replied Jean.

Chapter III

Jean is Second

W E had, for various reasons, changed our programme of races slightly by now although our basic plan remained the same. We had not run at the Vintage Car Club, Silverstone Meeting, for instance, because I discovered at the last moment that my membership of that Club had expired and it was not possible to rejoin again in time to have entries accepted for this particular meeting.

There was another date announced by the West Hants and Dorset Car Club—Whit-Monday, May 29th—for an excellent programme of races to be held at the new Blandford circuit and as their programme included a fifteen-lap race for Production Sports Cars, we put in an entry for this and received acceptance. Our plan was to run at the B.A.R.C. Meeting at Goodwood on Saturday, May 27th, and to spend the week-end at Bournemouth, as practice for the Blandford race was scheduled to take place on Sunday the 28th.

We also decided to put in entries for the meeting to be run at Silverstone by the Maidstone and Mid-Kent Club on June 10th, and for the meeting organized by the Midland Motoring Enthusiasts Club on July 1st, as these dates filled in gaps in our programme as compiled to date.

Our next race meeting therefore was the Goodwood Whit-Saturday Meeting, practice for which was scheduled for Friday, May 26th, and that day was one to remember, both from our own angle and for many thousands of other motorists, for it was while waiting in the paddock on that Friday morning that we heard that petrol had at last been taken off ration. At first one could hardly believe it after so many years of stringent rationing accompanied with the direst penalties for any infringement of the regulations.

At any rate it was going to make things a whole heap easier for us because, up to now, we had had to manage to race on the basic ration of the Healey alone. Now, however, we could race where we liked, as often as we liked and in as long races and as many races as we liked without the ever-present worry as to whether fuel supplies would hold out. We could also take another car as tender to the main meetings which we had not been able to do so far owing to the fuel shortage, and this was a tremendous help because it is amazing how much impedimenta one takes to a motor-race meeting when competing. Yes, the end of rationing meant a great deal to us and to tens of thousands of others.

In point of fact, I have never been a believer in wearing the car out with long practice sessions. I have never, at any time practised on any circuit without having every one of my practice laps timed on the watch by a member of my pit staff and, in addition, I always try to time every other competitor in any race in which I am running. Only in this way, to my mind, can one assess one's chances in a race and only in this way can one really get the very best results from the car, and it amazes me, when talking to other competitors, to see how few have an accurate idea of what results they are achieving in practice.

My own method is very simple and in my case, at any rate, works well. I always try to practise at a different time to competitors in my race so that, when they are practising, I can myself procure their times to compare with my own. I always prefer to practise as early as possible so that, if trouble does arise with the car, there is plenty of time to put it right. Each race or group of races is usually allocated a practice period of about an hour at small meetings, and by looking round the paddock beforehand it is usually possible to see whether one's principal rivals are likely to be out on the circuit towards the beginning or the latter part of the period. Assuming that my own car is ready to go out either at the beginning or the end of the period I always prefer to go out at the beginning provided my rivals are not all out at the same time.

When practising myself I have an arrangement with my own timekeeper that I stay out on the circuit so long as my lap times continue to improve. As soon as there is no longer any improvement I receive a signal whereupon I bring the car in and do not take it out again unless there is some very good

"*Warmed up and ready to go*"
JERSEY INTERNATIONAL ROAD RACE, JULY, 1950

"*The H.W.M. was still going as well as ever*"
JERSEY INTERNATIONAL ROAD RACE, JULY, 1950

37

[Photo : Guy Griffiths]

"A scratch start in a race full of men"

GOODWOOD, AUGUST, 1950

38

reason or unless I subsequently think of some method of improving the lap time already achieved. On circuits at which I run regularly, I usually find that four or five practice laps only are necessary if one is racing fairly frequently, and even on circuits on which I have never raced before I seldom do more than ten practice laps unless the circuit is a very long one or is, in some other respect, very tricky.

By now, we had found that a respectable lap for the Healey at Goodwood was two minutes dead when running on Pool petrol. We had been down to 1.58 when trying very hard or when following another car that was slightly faster, but as a general rule we would put the car away as soon as we had achieved a practice lap of two minutes or under.

At the Goodwood Whitsun Meeting we were running the car in one five-lap handicap race in which there were eighteen entries ranging from G. Jason Henry's 3½-litre Delahaye to the two tiny Fiats of F. J. Ames and A. H. Ellis. Adopting our usual tactics I soon found that our chances on handicap in this race were not awfully good. For instance, we were to start one minute and ten seconds before the scratch man, J. H. Goodhew's Monoposto Alfa-Romeo, together with Victor Hern on the tremendously fast 1,100-c.c. supercharged Amilcar, so ably prepared by Owen Finch and with R. A. Anderson's dark-blue Healey "Silverstone." Anderson had not raced at Goodwood before and he and I went out for practice together, his assistants kindly agreeing to time us both because I was without a timekeeper on this occasion.

Hern went out a little later than we did and had not done many laps before he had got his time down to 1 min. 56 secs., a speed of 74.5 m.p.h. against my 1.58, representing 73.2 m.p.h. Goodhew on the other hand was clocking 1.55 according to my watch, a time which would certainly not bring him into the picture unless he could improve upon it substantially. When practice concluded I had reached the conclusion that the race lay between Hern on the Amilcar, J. C. Byrom on an old 2.3 Bugatti, or possibly C. G. H. Dunham, despite his rather fearsome handicap in view of previous successes, although I had not been able to get a watch on E. J. Haesendonck, whose supercharged M.G. appeared to be going very well, or on G. A. Ruddock's H.R.G.

On race day the two little Fiats were non-starters, but everyone else to whom we had to concede start appeared to get
away well. At the fall of the flag, Hern on the Amilcar
absolutely streaked away from both Anderson's Healey and
my own. The acceleration of the Amilcar was terrific, but
as soon as we got on to the twisty section of the course, the
Healey began to score heavily. I estimated that Hern had got
between 50 and 60 yards lead from me when we went into
Madgwick Corner on the first lap, but between Madgwick and
Lavant Corners the Healey had regained it nearly all, due to
its tremendously superior road-holding and suspension. The
Amilcar scored again in acceleration along the Lavant straight
but its brakes did not appear to be so very good and I was
able to regain a few more of the yards I had lost on the straight
in the braking on the approach to Woodcote Corner. Out of
Woodcote Corner the Amilcar's acceleration told again and
I was having to work my very hardest to keep up but once we
were again on the section between Madgwick and Lavant it was
much easier. The contrast between the two cars on this
section was really quite remarkable. Victor Hern appeared to
me to be having the most uncomfortable ride of all time. The
smallest bump on the inside of a bend, unnoticeable on the
Healey, would send the inside wheels of the Amilcar five or
six inches up in the air to be followed by a series of nasty little
slides as more bumps were encountered. At times the unfortunate Hern appeared to be permanently suspended three or
four inches above his seat while I myself enjoyed what was
virtually an armchair ride. Nevertheless, I was having to do
my utmost all the time in order to keep within striking distance
of the Amilcar and any hope I might have had of getting in
front had, by now, completely vanished. I could only sit
behind him and accept the position unless he should blow up—
and that was exactly what happened. To my great surprise
the Amilcar suddenly slowed in the Lavant straight on lap
three and in a second I was by. For a moment, despite my
sympathy for Hern, my hopes rose, only to sink again as I
looked in my mirror on the run out from Madgwick to find
Byrom's Bugatti and Haesendonck's M.G. a hundred yards or
so behind.

I had received 25 secs. start in five laps from the supercharged

Bugatti and if he had managed to pick up as much as this in the first three laps it was obvious that he would finish well ahead of me. Haesendonck was also going very well indeed and they both came by me towards the end of the Lavant straight on the fourth lap. When they had passed I took another look in the mirror to find another blue car, Jason Henry's Delahaye, astern and believing I was third at the time I then pressed on as hard as possible in order to try and stay ahead of the Delahaye for the one remaining lap. I was able to do this and finished in the belief that the finishing order was Byrom, Heasendonck, myself and Jason Henry only to find that we had none of us caught G. A. Ruddock who had won the race on his H.R.G. at the very creditable speed of 71.95 m.p.h. As the Healey was, of course, running on Pool and had put in a lap of nearly seventy-four miles an hour I was quite satisfied with my fourth place and was now looking forward to running the car in company with other production cars running on the same fuel in the fifteen-lap scratch race to be held at Blandford on the following Monday.

The West Hants and Dorset Car Club had amended their original Regulations and there was now no official practice period on Sunday the 28th, but there was official practice on Saturday afternoon the 27th or on Monday morning and, as we were running at Goodwood on Saturday, we should obviously have to do our official practice on Monday.

Competitors were allowed, however, to go round the course on their ordinary touring cars on Sunday and this was a great help to anyone like myself who had never raced on the circuit before. Accordingly therefore my wife and sister-in-law, Anne Summers, and I did ten laps of the circuit in our 1950 Morris Minor on Sunday afternoon, each lap taking us around five minutes.

The Club had been very unfortunate in having some bad accidents on the circuit at previous meetings and it had been said in some quarters that the course was a dangerous one. They had insisted, therefore, that every competitor should walk over that part of the circuit on which most of the accidents had occurred, and, furthermore, that they should sign a statement to the effect that they had done so.

The distance round the circuit was three miles, two hundred

and twenty yards and the starting and finishing point, together with the paddock, lay exactly half-way along the only real straight on the course. This straight was roughly a quarter of a mile long and ended in a gradual right-hand corner with an adverse camber leading into a steep downhill section followed immediately by an equally steep uphill climb with, at the same time, a gradual left-hand curve. Towards the top of the hill the curve straightened out and there was a dead straight section up a slight gradient which formed the approach to what was known as Anson Corner. Anson Corner was a forty-five degree right-hand curve and led through a built-up area to the fastest section on the circuit, a series of very fast right-hand bends, all slightly downhill with a wide grass verge on either side. This part of the course was roughly a mile in length and terminated at Engineers' Corner at which began the part of the circuit where most of the bad accidents had occurred. Engineers' Corner itself was a seventy-five mile an hour right-hand bend followed by a short straight leading to Cinema Curve, another right hander of about the same speed. The course continued in a gradual left-hand direction through another built-up area to Hood Corner which was a ninety degree right-hand bend leading back into the starting and finishing straight. The surface of the course was excellent for its entire length and it seemed to me that there was no justification whatever for it being called a dangerous circuit. There was a full two and a half cars width at the narrowest point of the course and while some of the circuit did run through built-up areas it was certainly no more dangerous than most Continental road-racing circuits and was, I thought, a great deal safer than many I had raced on with motor-cycles before the war.

There were obviously some points at which passing was inadvisable, and I think myself that it was a circuit on which efficient flag marshals were even more desirable than usual and everybody seemed to me to do their jobs admirably.

We duly arrived at the circuit as instructed at 9 a.m. on Monday only to find that official practice had been put off from nine-thirty until ten o'clock, and it was actually after that before we were able to get out on the circuit. The Production Car Race had attracted an excellent entry which was divided into three classes: cars up to 1,500-c.c., cars over 1,500-c.c. but under 2,500-c.c., and cars of unlimited capacity.

The one and a half-litre class was composed of M.G., H.R.G. and Morgan entries, while in our own class there were no fewer than six Silverstone Healeys, two of the Le Mans type Frazer-Nashs and a lone Riley entered by L. W. Barter. The two Frazer-Nashs were entered by Anthony Crook, who was driving himself, and E. J. Newton, whose car was being driven by D. Pitt, a driver who had achieved considerable success in past seasons with M.G. cars. The Healeys were entered and to be driven by R. A. Anderson, K. Watkins, C. H. Masters, Leslie Onslow Bartlett, Sir Francis Samuelson, the well-known driver of Cooper cars, and finally our own car. The Unlimited Class consisted of three Allards, two of which, to be driven by S. H. Allard and R. K. N. Clarkson, were the latest competition type J.2, while the third was an apparently standard coupé to be driven by P. Farquharson.

As only two cars could be started abreast owing to the comparative narrowness of the circuit, the Club had very wisely dropped the Ballot system of determining starting positions and had adopted the Continental method of putting the entries who had achieved the best practice times in the front rows and it was therefore most important to make an all-out effort to put in a good practice lap. There was a board in the paddock on which the fastest times recorded in practice on the previous Saturday were shown. The fastest time of anyone had been put up by Anthony Crook who had done a lap in 2 mins. 25 secs., while Pitt on the other Frazer-Nash had done 2.31. The next best time, according to the board, had been put in by Leslie Onslow Bartlett who had been round in 2.38. The Allards had not yet practised and would, we thought, be able to get round much faster than we should and so we were aiming at Leslie Onslow Bartlett's time as we felt sure that we could not hope to compete with the Frazer-Nashs, which were both considerably lighter and, of course, much more expensive in consequence.

In order to put in a good lap we felt that it was important to get out on the circuit before it got crowded and we were waiting at the gate for nearly an hour so as to be sure of being first out on the circuit. The long wait paid us a good dividend because when the course was opened, we were able to put in six practice laps without seeing any sign of another car, although we knew that there had been a long queue of cars waiting behind us in the paddock. My wife and sister-in-law were signalling my practice times to me on a blackboard and these read as follows: 2.45, 2.39, 2.36 and 2.35. On the last of these laps I had been passed by S. H. Allard whose best practice lap was subsequently quoted as 2.31 and as I felt that we could not hope to improve substantially on these times I came in content to see what our fellow-competitors were doing.

It transpired that our lap of 2.35 was the fourth best practice time of the race and that only Crook, Pitt and Allard had done better. Accordingly, therefore, we found ourselves in the second rank at the start, Crook and Allard being ahead, Pitt in the same rank as ourselves and Onslow Bartlett directly astern. At the fall of the flag, the two Frazer-Nashs jumped into the lead, closely followed by Allard, ourselves fourth and Onslow Bartlett fifth. I soon found that it was not possible to hold the Frazer-Nashs and the Allard while driving within the bounds of safety and found also that I had no difficulty in maintaining my position ahead of Onslow Bartlett whose car appeared to be quite a bit slower than mine, but whose driving had to be seen to be believed. Time and time again I would take a corner at a speed that appeared to me to be creditable, only to find that Leslie had gained a dozen yards which I, in turn, would pick up in the long fast stretch between Anson Corner and Engineers' Corner. After we had done about six or seven laps, Leslie appeared to be dropping back slightly and seeing, as I thought, an opportunity of saving the Healey I reduced the revs in gears, going up to 4,500 out of Anson and Hood Corners instead of 4,800 r.p.m. Almost immediately Leslie's blue Healey appeared again astern and I had only just increased speed again when we began to lap the back markers of the 1,500-c.c. class which had started a minute behind us. I now discovered that I must keep going hard because if I was held up, even for a few seconds while passing a slower car, the blue Healey would appear ominously closely in my mirror until I had the feeling that, given a lucky break, he might well be able to slip by.

Meanwhile, developments had been taking place ahead for,

unknown to me, Allard had retired with a blown gasket, thus letting me into third place and Leslie to fourth while Crook was far from happy with both clutch and brake trouble, and Pitt on the other Frazer-Nash was holding a comfortable lead which he was never to lose.

At this stage we had covered twelve out of the fifteen laps and, for me, the sole remaining incident occurred when I was about to pass R. E. Molyneux on the downhill stretch out of Cuckoo curve. At this point of the course, if one is to take the subsequent uphill section fast, it is absolutely essential to hug the nearside grass verge closely because the downhill and uphill sections both form part of a very fast left-hand bend. With Onslow Bartlett closely behind me I came round Cuckoo Corner to find the T.C. M.G. tight into the left verge and I realized at once that if he stayed there I could not possibly get by before the blue Healey was upon us both. As Molyneux was already into the bend I could not see how he could possibly give way to me or how he could even know I was there, but, to my great surprise, he very sportingly eased off and somehow pulled over to the offside, giving me a perfect road which I took. It was a most considerate gesture and one which was of the greatest help to me and which, in my opinion, was synonymous with the general standard of driving in this race. All the drivers at this meeting had been addressed by Earl Howe before the race in view of the serious accidents at previous meetings and I think that considerable credit is due, particularly to the drivers of slower cars, that not one serious accident occurred in any race that day.

The race was won by Pitt in the Frazer-Nash, who covered the fifteen laps in 37 mins. 1.8 secs. at an average speed of 76.33 m.p.h., Anthony Crook was second in 37 mins. 14.4 secs. averaging 75.85, while our car was third, our time being 38 mins. 55.6 secs. equal to an average of 72.61 m.p.h. Leslie Onslow Bartlett was fourth, his time being 39 mins. 1.6 secs., and he was followed by Anderson, Masters' car driven by Stone and Sir Francis Samuelson. Healeys, therefore, finishing third, fourth, fifth, sixth and seventh, which we felt reflected great credit on the marque.

We ourselves were very pleased with our third place, although I am afraid that the race lacked interest from a spectator's point of view, this being sometimes unavoidable and unforeseeable.

But if our Production Car Race at Blandford lacked interest, that was to be compensated for at the Maidstone and Mid-Kent Race Meeting at Silverstone on June 10th.

As I had run the car at Goodwood and at Blandford and as Jean had not had a drive at either of those meetings, it was agreed between us that she should have all the driving on June 10th. The Maidstone and Mid-Kent Club had not included a class for 3-litre sports cars and so we entered the car for, what seemed to us to be the two most suitable classes, the 5-lap scratch race for sports cars up to four litres and the Unlimited Sports Car scratch race over the same distance. We had a glorious run up to Silverstone in the Healey and by the time we arrived in the paddock it was a sweltering hot day.

We had not seen a programme until we arrived on the course and so we had no idea of what competition we should meet. We found that the Unlimited Race was to be run before the race for cars up to four litres and that we had more or less the same opposition in each, although Mrs. Nancy Binns was not running her very fast 1½-litre Riley in the latter. Apart from Mrs. Binns, the principal menaces were various 2½- and 3½-litre Jaguars, Allards, another Silverstone Healey, some very fast Frazer-Nash B.M.W.s, and most formidable of all, Guy Gale in his tremendously fast 4-litre Darracq, which had been raced in turn by Ian Connell, Leslie Johnson, and, of course, by Gale himself with very considerable success.

We found in practice, as we had known, that the Darracq was far and away the fastest car at the meeting, although strong competition was being given by Gilbert Tyrer's very fast Frazer-Nash B.M.W., with whom we had had such a good scrap at Goodwood earlier in the season, and also by Oscar Moore's O.B.M. which was motoring better than we had ever seen it. We were allowed two practice sessions of three laps each, including one standing lap, and our times were as follows:—2 mins. 17 secs. (standing), 2.4 and 2.2 on our first session and 2.11 (standing), 1.59 and 1.58 on our second time out.

Against these times I recorded Guy Gale at 1.51, Tyrer 1.49, Moore 1.51, J. H. Craig's 3½-litre Jaguar 1.57, and Flt.-Lt. Stoop's streamlined F.N. B.M.W. 1.56. We had been watching Mrs. Binns with great interest following her excellent performances at Goodwood and elsewhere, and we were very sorry to hear from her that she had had engine trouble on the previous day and was not very hopeful about her chances. At this meeting, as at many of the Club meetings, it was possible to put in additional entries almost on the post, particularly if the event for which one wished to enter was poorly supported. Accordingly, therefore, we found that there were many last-minute entries in each of our races, and when we came up to the post for the Unlimited Sports Car Race there were a number of cars on the line that were not included in the programme.

The course in use for this meeting was not the Grand Prix Course but what is usually known as the Manufacturers Circuit. It is 2.278 miles in length and consists of a long straight of nearly 2,000 yards at the end of which there is a wide radius right-hand hairpin followed by a number of fast curves leading back into the long straight via another and tighter right-hand hairpin. As this latter bend was situated within 50 yards of the paddock and within 100 yards of the starting and finishing line, I decided to make it my vantage point for the meeting and on lap one of our first race I was amazed to see Jean holding second place behind the Darracq with two 3½-litre Jaguars scrapping for third place and the rest of the field stringing out behind. Although I had been able to see from my vantage point that she had made an excellent start I had certainly not expected her to be anywhere near as high up as this at the end of the first lap for, remember, this was only the second race in which she had ever run. As a matter of fact, I was so staggered that, for the moment, I forgot my duties as timekeeper and manager. I knew that there was no point in measuring the margin between Guy Gale and the Healey because I realized that that was bound to get bigger but, in practice, the Jaguars had also been faster than we. Yet, when I checked the margin between the leading Jaguar and our car I found that it was increasing by over a second per lap and before I had had time to get over my surprise, the race was over, having been won by Guy Gale at

73.08 m.p.h., with my wife second and H. T. Wilson's 3½-litre Jaguar third.

I was more than delighted for, on talking over the race afterwards, I realized that Jean had really driven with her head. Realizing that she could not compete with the Darracq with its vastly greater speed she had found that she could stay fairly comfortably ahead of everything else in the race, and this was exactly what she had done. The result was that, without unnecessarily straining the car, we had achieved as good a result as we could ever have hoped for.

At this stage of the proceedings competitors were being invited to put in additional entries, and we therefore entered for the Unlimited Racing Class which had not, up to that time, been well supported. On the line we found that many others had done the same with the result that we found ourselves in the midst of a motley array of cars ranging from 500-c.c. and 1,000-c.c. Coopers to genuine, dyed-in-the-wool Vintage machines. By now, I was prepared for almost anything and I was not surprised, therefore, to find a battle in progress between Oscar Moore and Gilbert Tyrer with our Healey in fourth place, sandwiched between a Cooper and the neat little 500-c.c. Emeryson, driven on this occasion by a neighbour of ours, Frank Kennington. On lap two, the Cooper approached the bend where I was watching too fast and spun round right in the path of our car which let Jean into third place and thinking that she was again in a place with no more serious opposition and no hope of catching the leaders, Jean once more dropped her maximum revs down to 4,500 in gears. Alas, we had miscalculated the determination of G. W. Wicken, the driver of the Cooper who had spun round, for he immediately restarted his car and set off in full flight. I had decided to sit in the stands for a change and was therefore unable to get down on to the circuit in time to give Jean a signal to go faster. Her lap-speed had dropped from 1.56 to 2.5 and I realized that at this rate Wicken must beat her into third place. This race was over a distance of seven and not five laps. Jean spotted her error on lap five when she found the Cooper again coming up astern in her mirror. Speeding up, she was able to hold him off until the start of the last lap but could not possibly retain her third place; Wicken finished third while the race was won by Oscar Moore at 76.60 m.p.h., with Tyrer second and our car fourth.

There was little doubt in our minds that we had thrown away a place in an endeavour to save the car. The responsibility rested fairly and squarely on my shoulders for I was, by agreement between us, the one who gave the orders and had I been doing my job it would never have happened. All credit was due to Wicken for restarting his car to regain his place, but we felt that we had really learnt something and made cast-iron plans there and then to prevent such a thing happening again.

The last race for sports cars up to 4-litre unsupercharged and $2\frac{3}{4}$-litre supercharged produced an enormous field of first-class quality, and proved by far the most exciting of the day, although, for some, it was a catastrophe.

At the end of the first lap the order was Gale, Moore, Tyrer, Victor Hern on the Amilcar, Willis, my wife, Stoop and W. Freed, on another Silverstone Healey, all tightly bunched together with my wife in the thickest part of all. I was watching on the inside of the same bend and was gratefully receiving reassurance from Bob Gerard who was watching at the same point and who was a Steward of the meeting as well as a Vice-President of the Club.

On the second lap Gale and Moore had got an appreciable lead on Tyrer, somewhat to my surprise, while Willis had disappeared leaving Hern in fourth place, Jean fifth with both Stoop and Freed right on her tail. On lap three, Tyrer dropped out, putting everyone behind him up one place, while on lap four I was not in the least surprised to find that Stoop was now in front of my wife. I had tried to impress on her that these Club meetings were a training ground for more important races elsewhere and that under no circumstances must she attempt to gain or maintain a place or attempt any manœuvre whatever unless she was absolutely sure that she had a substantial margin of safety.

On the last lap Gale appeared with Oscar Moore right on his tail, then there was a small gap and Hern appeared with Stoop on the streamlined Frazer-Nash B.M.W. and the two Healeys driven by my wife and Freed right behind him. I had a nasty feeling that something was going to happen for Stoop was approaching the bend at tremendous speed, apparently

intending to try and pass Hern. Half-way into the bend he got
into a terrific slide and the car turned right round travelling
backwards at about 70 m.p.h. To my horror I saw that Freed
was trying to pass my wife on the outside and I knew at once
that a fearful crash was virtually unavoidable, because I
estimated that at this point Freed was coming into the corner
at over 80 m.p.h.—an absolutely impossible speed at which to
take a bend like this. Fortunately for us, Jean was on the
inside of Freed or she must inevitably have been drawn into the
mêlée. The net result of it all was that Freed crashed head
on into Stoop's car thereby demolishing the front end of both
cars very thoroughly. It was an extraordinary accident
because, in the first place, it had apparently been quite obvious
to everyone I spoke to on the bend that they had seen it
coming while the drivers concerned had not; and, secondly,
because both drivers, in my opinion, made separate mistakes,
for both were not trying to pass the same car.

At all events we were well out of it and I was certainly
prouder than ever of my wife's ability to keep her head and
concentrate on her driving in an emergency. She duly
continued to finish in fourth place, a driver who had certainly
learnt more than most in her fourth short motor race. Once
again, the Healey was running as well at the end of the
afternoon as it had been at the beginning but, in view of the
considerable mileage it had covered at its last three race
meetings, we decided to have it given a comprehensive service
before running it again at the B.A.R.C. Goodwood Members
Meeting on the following Saturday, June 17th. We found
nothing out of adjustment, even the tappets being within half
a thou. of their original setting although, as a precaution, we
did take the brakes up very slightly. The car was thoroughly
greased and the engine oil was changed, these items being the
sum total of the work done.

I now thought that the time had come when I should pay
another visit to the R.A.C. Competitions Dept. to check on
the position regarding the T.T. in September. On doing so I
found that, as I had anticipated, the event was by invitation
only and that prospective runners were expected to intimate
to the R.A.C. their desire to be invited, whereupon the Club,
if it thought fit, would duly issue an invitation. It seemed that

priority was to be given to manufacturers and I therefore got
in touch with the Donald Healey Motor Co. and suggested
that, as they would obviously be invited, they should enter
the car, nominating myself as driver and I was very pleased
indeed to hear that they were agreeable to this suggestion.

They were very busy indeed at this time, for in addition to
their production machines, they were preparing a new car for
the 24-Hour Race to be run at Le Mans on June 24th and 25th.
This was of very great interest because we were already
wondering what our racing programme should be in 1951,
and if the company were to go into production with this
machine, it might well prove the solution to our problem. The
car in question was a standard Healey Silverstone chassis with
certain modifications to the body and was powered by a six-
cylinder American Nash engine of 3.8 litres, modified with a
special manifold and two S.U. carburetters. It was to be
driven at Le Mans by Tony Rolt and Duncan Hamilton, and
we were, of course, watching its progress with very great
interest.

Meanwhile, we again made tracks down to Goodwood on
June 17th with our own car which we had entered this time
in two handicaps and in one scratch race. The handicaps, in
which my wife was to drive, were for cars of any capacity
whether supercharged or unsupercharged while my race was
for unsupercharged cars of up to $2\frac{1}{2}$-litre capacity. All three
races were for five laps over the 2.4-mile circuit and all three
had attracted good entries.

The weather was not by any means perfect although we
had had many worse days. There was a fairly stiff breeze and
the sun would break through for short intervals, although
just as our official practice period began the rain came down.

We could not just sit in our paddock stall while the time
ticked away so I practised first, only to find that while it was
raining hard on one side of the circuit, the other side was bone
dry. The twisty part of the course from Madgwick Corner
to Lavant Corner was absolutely dry, but it was raining hard
along the Lavant straight, at Woodcote Corner, and in the
paddock. I did about five laps and found the Healey very
stable indeed under these conditions although Woodcote

Corner was very slippery and my lap time was down to 2 mins. 1 sec. in consequence.

By the time I had completed my practice laps the rain had stopped and Jean took over after I had warned her about the rather unusual conditions. Even so, I was surprised to find that her first lap time was only just inside three minutes while her next lap of 2 mins. 15 secs. was followed by seven more, the best of which was 2 mins. 3 secs.

Back in the paddock, my poor wife explained the mystery of the first lap. She had approached Woodcote Corner fairly cautiously knowing, as she thought, the conditions. Finding them not as bad as she expected, she had opened up a moment too soon whereupon the car had taken complete charge and had spun round twice and had finished the manœuvre facing back along the Lavant straight. Poor Jean had been very much put out by the whole business and had very wisely decided on a longer practice session than usual in order to regain her rather shaken confidence.

She assured me that she now felt quite all right again, but drivers who have had this happen will probably recall the nasty feeling that it gives one on the first occasion. We spent the rest of the morning watching our rivals and trying, at the same time, to spot the winners.

My race was first in the programme and in it were the usual selection of Frazer-Nash B.M.W.s, Jaguars and Healey Silverstones backed by a Riley, a Lea-Francis and Anthony Crook's Frazer-Nash. I had earmarked Anthony as potential winner of this race on his practice form, and when I found that he and I were to start in the second rank I resolved to get on his tail as quickly as possible and to stay there as long as I possibly could. Immediately ahead of me in the front rank were A. S. Lusty's Silverstone Healey and J. K. B. Brise's Jaguar and, as the starting flag fell, both these cars go away well. Anthony Crook made a tremendous get away and within eighty yards of the starting line I was immediately behind him alongside Lusty and Brise. Imagine my astonishment when the Frazer-Nash, with no warning whatever, suddenly cut out completely and stopped at the approach to Madgwick Corner. I found myself completely boxed in with cars sweeping by on all sides and by the time I had disentangled myself there were at least half a dozen cars ahead of me. During that first lap I did all I knew to make up for the time I had lost, and at the end I found that I was lying second, over eight seconds behind the leader, R. F. Peacock, in his very fast Frazer-Nash B.M.W. My four flying laps according to my wife and sister-in-law, Anne Summers, were 1.57, 1.56, 1.55½ and 1.55 dead, but although these were the four best laps I had ever done with the car at Goodwood, I could make no impression whatever on Peacock who won at the very creditable speed of 73.67 m.p.h. and whose time for the five-lap race was 9 mins. 46.4 secs. My own time was officially given as 9 mins. 53.2 secs. equalling 72.8 m.p.h., and Peacock was officially credited with fastest lap in the race, his lap time being 1 min. 55 secs. dead and representing a speed of 75.10 m.p.h. Brise's Jaguar was third and N. D. Yates' Healey Silverstone fourth, their times being 10 mins. 37.4 secs. and 10 mins. 38.2 secs. respectively.

From my own point of view the race, apart from the start, was quite devoid of incidents and I doubt whether there would have been any difference in the result even if I had not been held up on the first lap, for Peacock had really got his car cracking and was driving it beautifully. According to our timing his standing lap was achieved in 2 mins. 3 secs. against mine of 2 mins. 9 secs. including the hold up but, even so I had never so far put in a standing lap of under 2 mins. 5 secs. and I think that, in any case, he would have won the race on the standing lap alone.

My wife, we found, was driving in two consecutive races, an arrangement which would not suit everyone although it suited us admirably because, having studied the form carefully, we came to the conclusion that her chances were not at all bad in the second race, although they were, we felt, pretty hopeless in the first. So we decided to use the first of her races mainly as a " warmer up " for the second. All the " king pins " were in the first event and our entry was down to receive 41 secs. start from Guy Jason Henry in the big Grand Prix Delahaye over the five laps, 36 secs. from Guy Gale in the Darracq, 6 secs. only from Anthony Crook, while she had to *give* 14 secs. to Peacock, a concession we both knew she could not possibly make. The limit man, J. A. Williamson on a fine old 3-litre Bentley, was to receive 2 mins. 25 secs. from the Delahaye, and although there were one or two non-starters, everyone got away well.   After only a couple of laps, J. H. Craig emerged as an obvious winner, barring accidents, and he was duly followed home by Peacock, Anthony Crook, M. P. Rosen on a 2½-litre Jaguar, Guy Gale and Guy Jason Henry, who beat Jean into sixth place by a short head.   Her five-lap speeds had been 2 mins. 8 secs. (standing), 2 mins. 1 sec., 2 mins. 3 secs., 2 mins. 2 secs., and 2 mins. 2 secs. by my timing.

On returning to the paddock there was no time to discuss points before she was again sent out on a preliminary lap for her next race so I made my way to the starting line where I met her to " brief " her afresh.   There was really not much to say, but I wanted to remind her not to start the engine too soon as it was already well warmed up from the previous race.   In addition, I had by that time procured a list of non-starters from which I was able to tell her that, as the scratch man, Nigel Mann on the big supercharged Alfa-Romeo, was not starting, she and Miss P. M. Lambert on one of the very fast Lester M.G.s would be virtually starting from the scratch mark.   There being no one starting behind her, I thought it would help her to know how many people were ahead of her, because she could then know her exact position in the race as she caught and passed each car ahead, assuming, of course, that she could catch them.   Finally, I had to remind her that, in her previous race she had " crept " on the starting line before the flag had actually fallen and I told her that in the event of her being placed in a race in which she had done this at the start, she would almost certainly be penalized and might well find that her finishing position was discredited.

By the time I had got all this off my chest, the starter's flag was raised and the limit man, W. B. G. Leith, was away on his very smart cream M.G. to be followed in due course by the rest of the field.   The last two cars to depart before our own were the 1,750-c.c. supercharged Alfa-Romeos of A. H. Montague and J. Spindler, and 24 secs. after Spindler's car had departed the flag dropped for the Healey.

Jean got the car off the mark well, without any " creeping " and was almost at once ahead of Miss Lambert in the M.G. My watches were ticking away relentlessly and at the end of the first lap I found that she had done a first-class standing lap

time of 2 mins. 5 secs. By this time I had got up to my perch
on the balcony of the Members Bar, which is actually on the
outside of the circuit and is a point from which one can view
the proceedings almost all the way round the circuit. Almost
immediately, it seemed, the Healey was round again, now
rapidly overhauling some of the middle markers. I looked at
my watch and could not at first believe my eyes. One minute,
fifty-six seconds dead! It was not possible or, at any rate, I
could not believe it to be possible. " I'm afraid this blasted
watch has gone up the spout," I said to Jean's sister Anne. " I
don't think she could possibly have put in a lap at that speed,
particularly after the ' spin round ' this morning," and together
we studied the watch carefully. But it looked right and it was
right for the next lap was reeled off at one fifty-five, which left
us both pretty well speechless. At the end of this third lap the
Healey came past the stands in the process of passing one of the
blown Alfas, and half-way through the fourth lap Jean was
bearing down on and passing the M.G. driven by Leith to
which she had conceded 1 min. 19 secs. start.

" If she keeps this up, she must win it," I said to Anne, but
it was not to be, for on her last lap poor Jean got well and truly
boxed in amongst the limit men and it became obvious that
she could not hope to catch J. Goodhew, whose $4\frac{1}{2}$-litre
Lagonda was going great guns and was already in the lead.
There seemed a chance that she might be able to catch D. D.
Render's 4-litre Allard if she could get disentangled in time,
and this she very nearly did. She could not quite make it,
however, and finished 1.4 sec. behind the Allard who, in turn,
finished 13 secs. behind Goodhew, the winner. The Lagonda's
winning speed was 70.98 m.p.h., but as I arrived at our paddock
stall to congratulate my wife on her third place I was delighted
to hear the announcer say that the fastest lap of the race had
indeed been put up by our Healey at 75.10 m.p.h. or
1 min. 55 secs.

The scene at our stall was most encouraging and most
unusual at a Members Meeting. Autograph-hunters and well-
wishers besieged my wife and we were both delighted to find
Mr. Gordon Barker, the General Manager of the Donald Healey
Motor Co., amongst the throng. We were particularly pleased
that the car had gone well on the occasion of his visit, because,

E

although we had not at any time received or asked for any direct assistance from the manufacturers, we had at all times received the shrewdest advice together with great enthusiasm and co-operation, all of which had, of course, encouraged us tremendously.

We now had no more meetings until the beginning of July and, as the end of June marked the conclusion of another era in our ownership of the Healey, for we had by then completed our first three months of racing with the car, we reviewed the position generally and examined the results in relation to the finance we had outlaid.

We found that from the beginning of April until the end of June, we had entered for eleven races and in one only had we failed to start. That was, of course, the first of all, at Goodwood on Easter Monday, when we suffered fuel-feed trouble. Of the remainder, Jean had run in six and had achieved one second place, one third, two fourths, one fifth, and one seventh places, while I had run in four races and had managed two seconds, one third and a fourth. With the exception of the Blandford Production Car Race, all these had been races over a distance of twelve miles or less and the car had never been placed lower than fourth in a scratch race, the average number of starters throughout being twelve exactly. I had driven mainly in the scratch races because we both felt that as I had, until now, been slightly the faster that was the way most likely to produce the best results. Nevertheless, we were quite unable to follow the handicappers' reasoning in most of Jean's short handicap races and we now resolved to do as few handicap races as possible in the future.

On the financial side the position was that we had received £20 in bonus from accessory manufacturers at the beginning of the season and had received £15 13s. from the organizers of the Blandford Races in respect of our third place in the Blandford Production Car Race. Total £35 13s.

Against this, we had spent £28 1s. in Club Subscriptions and Entry Fees, £18 19s. on tyres, £9 18s. on fuel, £9 10s. on maintainance of the car, and £5 15s. on equipment. Total £72 3s.

The greater part of the sum spent on maintainance of the car was in respect of our fuel-feed trouble at Easter, while the sum of £5 15s. represented the purchase price of two crash helmets. I had been trying to persuade Jean to wear a crash helmet for a long time but as I had not got one myself I was obviously on weak ground. Finally, however, Nemesis overtook me for, arriving at the Blandford Meeting without having read the regulations properly, I found that crash hats were compulsory. If it had not been for the kindness of Peter Clark who lent me his, I should very probably have been unable to start. Obviously, therefore, we had reached a point where the purchase of two crash helmets could no longer be delayed.

The position, therefore, appeared to be that, having deducted our income from our expenditure, our three months' fun had cost us £36 10s., a figure which we could only regard as really small in relation to the great pleasure we had had from the car. I am no accountant and one can obviously go very much more deeply into the thing, detailing hotel bills, depreciation on the car and other angles, but the figures I have given were the ones that interested me and will, I hope, be of interest to readers of this book.

CHAPTER IV

I Go to Jersey

THE second half of our racing season began with another meeting of short races at Silverstone, organized this time by the Midlands Motoring Enthusiasts' Club. We had again entered the car in a handicap and a scratch race but, on receipt of the official programme, try as we would, we were quite unable to follow the officials reasoning in the handicap in which Jean was to drive. Bearing in mind that our best lap to date on this circuit was 1 min. 56 secs., and that this was also the best lap time achieved on this circuit by a Silverstone Healey so far, we found that we had been given 3 secs. start per lap from Gilbert Tyrer who had put in an official lap in under 1 min. 40 secs. only a few weeks previously. In addition, we had to give 9 secs. *per lap* to Chevell's Alvis, Downing's Connaught and Rowley's Aston Martin; 11 secs. *per lap* to Mrs. Binns' Riley, Mansell's Allard and Radford's Riley and 13 secs. *per lap* to Ruddock's very fast H.R.G. and Taylor's 3½-litre Jaguar. We had certainly not expected to be given a race but we had hoped to be given a chance. As it was we were literally handicapped right out of it and we just could not see on what basis the handicap had been worked out.

However, Jean was very keen to run and so we decided to make the best of it although we were beginning to feel that we might do better to stick to scratch races only. Jean had run on this circuit before and so I had first practice and gradually improved in about six laps to 1.57 secs. Jean then went out and quite quickly got down to 1 min. 55 secs., and as there was still some of the practice period left I had another crack and managed to improve to 1 min. 54 secs.

As my race was at 3.15 p.m. and Jean's handicap was not until 4.50 p.m. we decided to take a trip in the car in order to watch the preceding races from the farther end of the course, and this nearly proved disastrous from my point of view. We had watched the first four races from a good vantage point on the course, my own race was the sixth and we were debating whether to watch one more or whether to return in very good time to the paddock. We decided at last to return and on reaching the paddock we were pounced on by our respective paddock marshal who told us, breathlessly, that Race No. Five had been postponed owing to lack of entries and that the starters for Race No. Six were on the line and about to start. There was no time to be lost, and grabbing a pair of goggles and a helmet I motored to the starting line hot-foot to find that I was, in fact, just in time to rank as a starter.

On paper the race did not appear to be one in which the opposition was very formidable with the sole exception of Tyrer with whom I knew I could not cope. We had come out on top against B. Chevell's Alvis and Le Fever on the other Silverstone Healey at previous events and although I had not run against J. W. Rowley's 2-litre Aston Martin I felt that on our respective practice times that I should be able to beat him. As I had anticipated, Tyrer took the lead with ease but I certainly hadn't anticipated the terrific scrap that developed for second and third places between Chevell, Rowley and myself. I must admit that prior to the start of the race I had anticipated a fairly easy second place, but any illusions I had on that score were very quickly shattered. At the end of the first lap I lay second to Tyrer but at the beginning of the second lap the scrap really began. First Chevell would lead for half a lap, then I would get ahead, and on one occasion Rowley passed us both at the exit from the straight, only to find that he had approached the hairpin too fast and was partially out of control, thereby having to drop back again to fourth place. So it went on for the whole six laps, Chevell finishing second, myself third and Rowley fourth. It was certainly a marvellous scrap and was, to me, an object lesson in not counting your chickens before they hatch, for right until the finishing flag was in sight, second place might have fallen to any one of the three of us.

Now we could really see how poor the handicapping was, for in her race, Jean had to give these two drivers 57 secs. in six laps while the unfortunate Le Fever who had not been in the running in the scratch race was called on to do the same although, for some unknown reason, G. A. T. Weldon's Healey Silverstone, which was identical to Le Fever's and our own, was sent off the same mark as Rowley and Chevell.

Jean did everything possible and did, in fact, improve on her practice time by nearly a second, but as we already knew, to no avail. The race was won easily by D. O. Taylor's $3\frac{1}{2}$-litre Jaguar off the limit mark, Ruddock's H.R.G. being second and Rowley on the Aston Martin, third. Our Healey finished eleventh, while Le Fever was thirteenth and last.

We now had a lull in the proceedings and, according to the programme we had mapped out at the start of the season, there were no more meetings due until the next Goodwood Club Meeting on August 12th.

My co-director, Alastair Baring had, meanwhile, had several good runs with his Formula 2 2-litre unblown H.W.M. and was entered for the Jersey International Road Race to be held on July 13th. I had planned to go with him in order to organize his pit arrangements, but as time wore on it became obvious that it was not going to be easy for us both to go, and on Monday the 10th we had a meeting to discuss what was to be done. We were exceptionally busy at that time and I was quite prepared to stand down myself and had already suggested it when, to my great surprise, Baring generously asked me if I would like to take over the entry and drive in his place.

Needless to say, I required no second invitation and I accepted gratefully while stipulating that if I took the entry over I should take it, lock, stock and barrel, debit and credit. In other words, that I should take over the expense side, involving everything from hotel bookings to shipping charges for the H.W.M. and its racing van. I also undertook to pay for any damage I might do to the car, either to the engine or transmission or to any part of it as result of a crash. I was not greatly worried over the risk involved in the last two items because, mechanically, the H.W.M. had an excellent record and although I had not seen it, I had had the Jersey course described to me in considerable detail. The H.W.M., together with its van, driven by Baring's mechanic Buckle, was already in Jersey, having gone direct from France following the Formula 2 race run in conjunction with the French Grand Prix at Reims.

Practice for the Jersey race was scheduled to take place on Tuesday and Wednesday, July 11th and 12th in the evening, and as it was unlikely that I should get over in time for Tuesday's practice period, for I had quite a lot to clear up beforehand, I decided not to try, but to catch the Tuesday night boat from Southampton, arriving at Jersey between 9 a.m. and 10 a.m. on Wednesday.

I had got no bookings made so I immediately contacted our very good friend Mr. Bird of Autocheques in Regent Street who is, to my mind, an expert without parallel in arranging travel of the most awkward kind, at short notice. Bird's patience has to be seen to be believed when dealing with the problems of the motor-racing fraternity travelling abroad and I was right in thinking that he would not fail me here.

I left the office at Bracknell at 5 p.m. on Tuesday evening, therefore, and having collected Jean from home, we motored straight down to Southampton where we had dinner, garaged the car and boarded the boat which was due to sail at 11.45 a.m. We had just got on board when we met Angela Hamilton, wife of Duncan Hamilton, who was sharing the wheel of a 6C Maserati with his racing partner Philip Fotheringham Parker. Duncan and Philip had gone on ahead and were practising that evening and Angela was joining them in Jersey. We all made our way to the bar where we found Freddie Dixon of Riley fame, and just before the boat sailed we were joined by Tony Rolt who was driving the evergreen $1\frac{1}{2}$-litre straight-eight Delage that had been raced by Habershon in 1949.

From my point of view, the less said about the crossing the better because I am not the best of sailors, but suffice it to say that, on arrival at Jersey both Jean and I made our way straight to the Air Terminal where we cancelled our return boat passage and booked ourselves home by air. The Tuesday evening practice period had, we found, been quite uneventful, fastest practice time having been put up by David Hampshire in his Scuderia Ambrosiana 4CLT Maserati. This was one of six cars of this type, the others being driven by Louis Chiron, Franco Rol, Baron de Graffenried, Prince Bira and Reg Parnell. Another car of this type had been entered by Leslie Brooke, but this was a non-runner and its place and number being taken by T. Branca, driving a $1\frac{1}{2}$-litre unsupercharged Simca. The only other Maserati was the six-cylinder to be driven by Hamilton and Fotheringham Parker and there was one Ferrari which was to be driven by Peter Whitehead. E.R.A.s were being driven by Bob Gerard, Cuthbert Harrison, Graham Whitehead, Brian Shawe Taylor and Joe Ashmore, and in addition to the Delage to be driven by Rolt, there were two post-war Altas entered by Crossley and Kelly. Of these, Crossley's, which was the earlier car, had single-stage supercharging while Kelly's had two-stage. With the exception of Branca's Simca, all these cars were supercharged, but in addition to our H.W.M., which was, of course, a Formula 2, or 2-litre unsupercharged machine, there were three unsupercharged Coopers to be driven by W. S. Aston, R. W. Merrick and S. Logan, and A. J. Butterworth's $4\frac{1}{2}$-litre unsupercharged A.J.B.

The race was, of course, for Formula 1 cars of $1\frac{1}{2}$-litre supercharged or $4\frac{1}{2}$-litre unsupercharged capacity and, as our H.W.M. was an unsupercharged machine of only two-litre capacity, we were, of course, giving away two and a half litres straight away. We could not, therefore, hope to do any real good in the race unless a lot of the faster cars retired although Stirling Moss and Lance Macklin had produced some amazing results abroad when driving these little cars in similar races. We could obviously set ourselves a target, however, in endeavouring to be the first unsupercharged car to finish in the race and this we decided to do. We knew that the Coopers were all very fast and that Butterworth had a large number of successes to his credit in sprint events and we realized that Branca on the Simca might go very fast indeed.

As soon as we had recovered from the journey we located " Buster " Baring's mechanic who was waiting with the car in Jersey and made the necessary arrangements with him for practice that evening. We then had the car scrutineered and having emerged from this ordeal unscathed we decided to look round the town as we had neither of us been there before. Jean was entranced with the shops and the day went very quickly until practice time loomed ahead at six that evening.

We then made our way up to the pits to find Buckle with the car already unloaded from the lorry, and warmed up and ready to go. We found that we were not the only ones to have missed the first night's practice because both De Graffenried and Bira had only just arrived with their Maseratis, but Chiron and Rol had still not arrived and were not now expected. The Jersey driver Syd Logan was in considerable trouble with his Cooper and Butterworth, whose pit was next to ours, had had a lot of bother during the previous practice period and was apparently not yet out of it.

We had not to wait many minutes at our pit before the circuit was opened and by the time I had run over the various points of the car with Buckle we were given the O.K. by our respective pit marshal. The car was, by the way, fitted with a self-starter, although in view of the high compression-ratio of the engine this was not always a certain method of starting and on this first occasion we push-started in order to make sure that we did not wet or oil up a plug.

The method of starting was very simple, for the car was fitted with a four-speed self-change box. We push-started in third speed, again in view of the high ratio, and immediately the engine fired, we changed to first and then, of course, changed up through the gears normally. The car fired at once and got away perfectly cleanly. I had, of course, never been round the circuit before so I went very steadily for several laps before attempting to go at all fast.

I found the St. Helier circuit much easier to learn than I had anticipated mainly because the first half of the circuit is along the promenade and amounts to one tremendously fast full bore in top left-hand bend. The pits are at the West Park end, or start, of this and the course turns inland away from the promenade at Bell Royal Corner, a 90-m.p.h. right-hand turn, followed almost immediately by Le Marquands Corner, a 15-m.p.h. right-hand hairpin bend leading into the built-up return section to West Park Corner, another hairpin bend similar to Le Marquands but with a fairly steep downhill approach. The 1½-mile section from Le Marquands to West Park is all through streets of medium width, excellently surfaced and with one exception being a series of very fast left- and right-hand bends. The exception is Millbrook Corner, which I personally found the trickiest part of the course to learn, mainly because the approach is very fast and, as it is over the brow of a hill, completely blind. In other words, one approaches the corner which is a 75-m.p.h. right-hand bend at anything up to 115 m.p.h. without being able to see it until one is over the brow of the hill and then virtually into the corner. I should perhaps make the point that these speed figures are purely estimated ones which I have arrived at after having talked to other drivers in the race on the subject.

On the H.W.M. I found that the best way to deal with this particular bend was to approach the area full bore in top gear, having previously preselected third gear on the preselector box. One would go full bore over the brow of the hill and, as soon as the corner showed up, brake hard momentarily and change into third. The corner could then be taken full bore in third, after which one again got into top and stayed in top until arriving once again at West Park Pavilion and the start. Both the West Park and Le Marquands hairpins were, of course, first-gear bends.

We had had a chance to estimate what sort of lap times we should have to achieve by studying the lap times put in practice the previous evening by the Simca and the Coopers, and we decided that we could not feel that we were doing the car justice until we had got down to the 2 mins. 25 secs. to 2 mins. 15 secs. mark. Having done seven practice laps we were down to 2 mins. 24 secs. and I then came into the pits to review the situation with Jean and Buckle. The car was running faultlessly and although it was very different from the Healey from a handling point of view, its road-holding was so good that I had no difficulty whatever with it at any part of the course. The main points of difference from the Healey were, first of all, complete lack of roll on corners of the H.W.M. due, I imagined, to its weight being so very much less, and secondly, the much greater surge of power of the H.W.M. on opening the throttle.

The former point was to be expected because the Healey was essentially a sports car carrying full road equipment and was far in excess of any other car of its class that I had tried, particularly from the point of view of handling, although its comparatively high weight sometimes left it at a disadvantage on acceleration from other cars which were considerably lighter and more costly.

Otherwise, the H.W.M. was in every way similar to any other very fast sports car I had driven and I felt, at once, that it should prove an extremely pleasant machine to drive in a race of this sort. Having found how our time compared with the other cars of similar capacity I went out again to do a few more laps and by the time the practice period was over we had got our time down to 2 mins. 18 secs., and I felt sure that I could improve upon this in the race. The car was still motoring perfectly and as we had now done fifteen laps, we decided to put it away.

We filled it up with fuel therefore and Buckle took it back to the garage in order to give it a final check over while I went to find out what were the highlights of this practice period. I found that the Club had already got out the starting positions for the race next day, based on the best practice time done by each competitor in either practice session and this worked out as follows :

Front Row.—D. Hampshire (Maserati) 94.12 m.p.h. ; P. N. Whitehead (Ferrari) 93.51 m.p.h. ; F. R. Gerard (E.R.A.) 92.6 m.p.h. ; T. C. Harrison (E.R.A.) 92.31 m.p.h.

Second Row.—De Graffenried (Maserati) 91.87 m.p.h. ; B. Shawe Taylor (E.R.A.) 91.58 m.p.h. ; R. Parnell (Maserati) 90.14 m.p.h.

Third Row.—A. P. Rolt (Delage) 89.72 m.p.h. ; J. Kelly (Alta) 89.44 m.p.h. ; B. Bira (Maserati) 88.89 m.p.h. ; D. Murray (Maserati) 86.75 m.p.h.

Fourth Row.—J. Ashmore (E.R.A.) 86.09 m.p.h. ; J. Duncan Hamilton (Maserati) 85.84 m.p.h. ; W. S. Aston (Cooper) 85.84 m.p.h.

Fifth Row.—T. Branca (Simca) 83.96 m.p.h. ; C. Mortimer (H.W.M.) 83.00 m.p.h. ; G. Crossley (Alta) 82.76 m.p.h.

Sixth Row.—A. G. Whitehead (E.R.A.) 82.64 m.p.h. ; R. W. Merrick (Cooper) 72.45 m.p.h.

I was reasonably satisfied with our practice speed of 83 m.p.h. because, in the first place, the car was not mine and I felt very responsible for its safe return to " Buster " Baring in good condition. Secondly, I had not seen the course before that evening and thirdly, I had never even sat in the car until that day. Nevertheless, I had no illusions as to how my performance would have compared with the other regular H.W.M. drivers, but I felt that the race was a fairly long one and that if the car was kept going at about that speed, and was still running at the finish, it would not disgrace itself.

Although the race was not due to start until 3 p.m. we were up early on the Thursday to find that although it was not actually raining, the weather was by no means perfect. Rain did actually fall later in the day and it still seemed likely to rain again up to about an hour before the start of the race. As we had had the car scrutineered without incident earlier in the day, we were up to the start in good time and had everything unloaded and laid out in the pit by half past two.

Having warmed the car up on an opening parade lap, I left it with Buckle who changed the plugs while, with the other drivers, I was introduced by Earl Howe to Lieut.-General Sir Edward Grasett, H.E. the Lieut.-Governor of the Island. Then I returned to the car to find everything ready to go. We knew that we should have to refuel and as the race was over 55 laps of the 3.2 mile circuit, we agreed that our fuel stop should take place some time after the thirtieth lap. The decision as to when to come in was to rest with me as soon as I had acknowledged a signal from the pit showing that we had completed our 30 laps. We had rehearsed our pit stop very carefully that morning and it had been agreed that Buckle and our assistant, from the garage where the car had been kept, should perform the actual refuelling while Jean should cover me with a rug to prevent my becoming soaked with fuel and should also give me a drink.

In no time at all, it seemed, the signals were being given for five, four, three, two and one minutes before the start and on the one-minute signal we drew the car back and push-started. It started perfectly to my great relief and was, I think, the first car to do so. Once the engine had started things were not quite so easy, for there was quite a bit of forward drag from the preselector box and I had to keep the brakes on while keeping the engine running in order to avoid running into the back of Duncan Hamilton's Maserati, which was directly ahead in row four.

The H.W.M. had a very high first-gear ratio and I had been warned previously not to attempt a quick start but to let the car get rolling before really giving it the gun. When the flag fell there was a tremendous surge forward and several cars in the rows directly ahead were bumping into one another for a fraction of a second until the mêlée sorted itself out. Along the promenade the field began to sort itself out but not as quickly as I had thought and as we went into Bel Royal and Le Marquands Corners we became just as bunched as we had been right at the start. Again, from the stretch from Le Marquands to Millbrook we began to space out, but almost immediately, it seemed, we were at West Park and still just as tightly bunched as ever. What was happening, of course, was that the field was dividing itself into two sections. The first section, consisting of the very fast boys, was already well ahead, while I had got myself in the middle of a group of cars travelling more slowly.

Having rounded West Park Hairpin I was able to take stock of my immediate neighbours. Just ahead was Branca on the Simca and ahead of him was Duncan Hamilton who was close on the tail of Graham Whitehead on the E.R.A., Shawe Taylor on another E.R.A. and Kelly on the two-stage super-charged Alta were still farther ahead and were disappearing rapidly while in the mirror I could see Geoffrey Crossley in the other Alta and farther astern, David Murray and Tony Rolt, both of whom had made bad starts. Next time past the pits, Tony Rolt came by at great speed and Crossley rather more slowly and as we went into Bel Royal I was able to pass Branca whereupon I glued myself to the tail of Duncan Hamilton's Maserati. Rather to my surprise, Murray who was on my tail did not pass and for four or five laps we continued like this, Murray finally passing both Duncan and me albeit very slowly indeed although as it went by me the car sounded quite healthy.

Duncan, meanwhile, was driving in his own inimitable style, fairly hurtling round the bends on the back stretch and together we continued for several laps, the Maserati having rather more " poke " out of the bends, the maximum of both cars appearing to be about the same while the H.W.M. scored heavily with its marvellous brakes. Lap after lap Duncan would pull away down the promenade but always I was able to get right on his tail again at Le Marquands and I began to think that I ought to try to get in front there. No sooner had I decided to try when Duncan went into Le Marquands a shade too fast, the car slid under the brakes, corrected, and slid again and before I had time to realize it, Duncan was motoring backwards alongside me. For a moment I braked hard because it looked to me as though I was right in the front row to get squashed between the Maserati and the wall, but Duncan, still working furiously, brought the car to a standstill in the middle of the road facing Bel Royal from whence it had come. I had no difficulty in filtering round the Maserati and I quickly pressed on for I wasn't sure whether or not Duncan had been able to keep the engine running. I now knew that both Branca, Duncan and Merrick on the other Cooper were astern and that I was not running last at any rate and as I was now motoring in a little pocket by myself and was not likely to overtake anyone I began to try and glean some information from the " dead car park " alongside the pits where the various retirements had been pushed. To my surprise I saw that there were already two Maseratis there while Tony Rolt was getting out of the Delage between Le Marquands and Millbrook shrouded by clouds of steam or vapour of some kind.

The H.W.M. was still going as well as ever and now I had another duty which was to keep well out of the way of the leaders, for we were being lapped for the first time. The order was, I found, Peter Whitehead on the Ferrari, followed by Reg Parnell and De Graffenried, both on 4CLT Maseratis. I had estimated that we would probably be lapped either five or six times by the winner and so from the tenth lap onwards I was kept quite busy keeping a watch out in the mirror for those overtaking. In a surprisingly short time, it seemed, our thirty-lap signal appeared and I decided to come in for fuel on lap 31. The only thing, in fact, that would have decided me to continue for the time being would have been a collection of other cars in at the pits near our own at that time, but as there were only two in, and both were at the opposite end, there was obviously no reason why we should not refuel right away.

As I pulled away from West Park and signalled that I was coming in I wondered how we would get on. Neither Jean, Buckle nor his assistant had ever refuelled a car during a race and I had never driven one that required refuelling although I had done so in motor-cycle races before the war. As I approached the pits I recalled vividly the snags and pitfalls of organizing a rapid and well drilled pit stop—the amazing ease with which one can overshoot the pit after travelling fast for some time—the ease with which attendants can collide unless their paths and actions have been carefully mapped out before-hand and their duties correlated and the chaos that can result if a fuel churn or oil drum is upset at the crucial moment. I hoped sincerely that neither of these things nor the other legion of catastrophes would befall us—and none of them did. The car came to rest dead opposite the pit in an atmosphere, from my own point of view, of dead silence and as it did so, I recalled " Buster's " last words before I left for Jersey : " The exhaust pipes of the car come to an end dead opposite your right elbow so, whatever you do, don't forget to plug your ears well and truly with cotton wool or you'll be deaf as hell when you stop ! "

Deaf I was and deaf I stayed in a gradually increasing degree until long after we had got home from Jersey. The fault was entirely mine because I had been warned and had not remembered to take the necessary action. Before I had had time fully to realize my bloomer, however, I was enveloped from head downwards in an enormous and, I thought, intolerably hot car rug, and a large glass of lemonade was thrust under it, half emptying itself into my lap as it arrived.   I just had time to grasp it and to start drinking it when, to my complete astonishment, both the rug and the lemonade were whisked from me and the car started to move, Jean's voice in the dim distance reminding me, " Steer it.   You're away."   Although we were only putting in five gallons, for we estimated that we should not need more, I was so staggered that for a moment I very nearly failed to " Steer it " and it was fortunate, perhaps, that at that moment the motive power was supplied by Buckle and not by the car's own power unit.   I soon grasped the situation and did my stuff, and the car was away again running just as cleanly as before.

As I got away from the pit Branca went by and I realized that if we were to achieve our aim of being the first unblown car to finish, I should have to get my skates on and catch up with him and pass him again.   I thought rapidly about the pit stop and for a moment, I confess, I wondered whether there had been some fearful mistake, everybody thinking that someone else was putting in the fuel and I was leaving the pit unfilled in consequence because, to me, the stop had seemed too quick and efficient to be true.   I watched, therefore, very very carefully in case I should be " urgently recalled " in the event of such a disaster being discovered, but as I received no signal I assumed either that the car would run out of fuel or that the necessary amount had, in fact, gone in.

I had little difficulty in catching up and passing the Simca again, the H.W.M. having a noticeably greater maximum speed although Branca certainly knew his car and clung behind tenaciously on the back leg of the course.   Soon we had reached the 40-lap mark and I began to try to estimate the numbers left in the race.   In the case of the first six or so it was not too difficult because they had been lapping me more frequently and I found I could memorize them, but there were some who had only lapped me once and for all I knew there were probably some who had not lapped me at all.   I had not seen Duncan again and assumed that he was still behind me, for I could not see the pale green Maserati stopped at any part of the course although I didn't rule out the possibility that either he

"Jean was able to get by Pycroft who was going great guns "
GOODWOOD, AUGUST, 1950

" In this case it did not really work "
GOODWOOD, AUGUST, 1950

F

" Buster took over in Race 8 "
GOODWOOD, AUGUST, 1950

" Since Jean was now driving so well "
GOODWOOD, AUGUST, 1950

or Philip Fotheringham Parker, to whom he was handing over at half distance, might well have gone by when I was enjoying my spell under the rug at the pits.

We appeared to be set to finish when, to my horror, the car missed a beat when leaving West Park. I assumed that, as the road had got rather slippery at that point, I had gone too slowly and had nearly juiced up a plug, but the same thing happened at Le Marquands and again at West Park on the next lap. What should I do ? I realized that, if I stopped to change a plug, and I could only assume that the trouble was a plug, I should certainly be passed by both Branca and Duncan Hamilton, assuming they were both running, although if I kept going for long under such conditions I might do the car considerable harm.

I signalled the pit to ask them to tell me my lap number and found that I was beginning my forty-eighth lap. The car was getting much worse as they could hear for themselves, and on looking in the mirror I was really shaken to find Branca already in sight astern. The race distance was, I knew, 55 laps and I was pretty sure that Peter Whitehead, who was still in the lead, had lapped me at least five times. As the entire field was to be flagged off as soon as the winner crossed the line it seemed to me that I should only have to do one or two more laps before I should be flagged off as a finisher. I decided, therefore, to keep cracking, for the Simca was now only three or four lengths astern.

At the end of lap 49 he was less than two lengths behind and the misfiring of the H.W.M. had become chronic and was happening at Bel Royal and Millbrook, as well as at the two hairpins, and as we came into West Park at the end of lap 50 I doubted whether I could hold him off until the finishing line, 200 yards after the corner, even if the finishing flag were given to us.

There was such an appalling time lag between the time one opened the throttle and the time the engine chimed in on all four that I decided to try opening up as I went into the corner in the hope that, by this means, the engine would start pulling when I was coming out of it. The Simca was now alongside when, to my chagrin, the engine of the H.W.M. chimed in

F*

long before I was ready for it, right on the apex of the corner. The car at once went into a powerful slide and for a moment I had a fine view of Branca and his Simca skimming the edge of my radiator grille before the H.W.M. straightened up and was away.

As soon as the car was straight I saw that the chequered flag was in fact being flown and we roared away from the hairpin absolutely neck and neck.   To my delight, the tactics I had adopted at West Park seemed to have worked, for the car cleared itself slightly earlier than it had on previous laps and crossed the line with the Simca barely one second astern.

On pulling up at the pits, everyone appeared to be talking although, to me, there was still complete and absolute silence. I could dimly hear the announcer's voice giving the official results, but he might have been announcing them in Chinese for all the sense it made to me.   People came up to talk to me, presumably about the race.   Their lips moved but I heard nothing and feeling a complete lemon I hurried away and back to the hotel for a bath.   I was surprised not to feel in the least bit tired, for I had done betwen 150 and 160 miles at an average of between 81 and 82 miles per hour according to my reckoning.   Neither had I any chafes nor bruises such as one so often discovers after many shorter races than this.   All this spoke very highly for the car and its designers, and having had my bath I was visited by Buckle displaying a carburetter float over half full of fuel.   So this had been our trouble and I was interested to hear that having changed the punctured float, the car started up and ran on all four cylinders immediately.

While I was dressing, a copy of the local paper which included a full report of the race was thrust under the door of our room and I found that, as I had anticipated, Peter Whitehead had had an easy win on the Ferrari, followed by Parnell and De Graffenried.   We had finished tenth behind Joe Ashmore's E.R.A. and ahead of Branca and Hamilton, the full finishing order being as follows :

1st.   No. 10.   P. N. Whitehead (Ferrari).   Time : 1 hr. 56 mins. 2.6 secs.   Speed :   90.94 m.p.h.

2nd.   No. 5.   R. Parnell (Maserati) 54 laps.   Time : 1 hr. 56 mins. 7.2 secs.   Speed : 89.30 m.p.h.

3rd.   No. 3.   Baron E. de Graffenried (Maserati) 54 laps.   Time : 1 hr. 57 mins. 7 secs.   Speed : 88.55 m.p.h.

4th.   No. 11.   F. R. Gerard (E.R.A.) 54 laps.   Time : 1 hr. 57 mins. 31.8 secs.   Speed : 88.22 m.p.h.

5th.   No. 15.   B. Shawe Taylor (E.R.A.) 54 laps.   Time : 1 hr. 57 mins. 57.4 secs.   Speed : 87.89 m.p.h.

6th.   No. 18.   G. Crossley (Alta) 51 laps.   Time : 1 hr. 56 mins. 30.2 secs.

7th.   No. 14.   A. G. Whitehead (E.R.A.) 51 laps.   Time : 1 hr. 56 mins. 37 secs.

8th.   No. 19.   J. Kelly (Alta) 51 laps.   Time : 1 hr. 57 mins. 16 secs.

9th.   No. 16.   J. Ashmore (E.R.A.) 50 laps.   Time : 1 hr. 56 mins. 7.4 secs.

10th.   No. 21.   C. Mortimer (H.W.M.) 50 laps.   Time : 1 hr. 57 mins. 40 secs.

11th.   No. 9.   T. Branca (Simca) 50 laps.   Time : 1 hr. 57 mins. 41 secs.

12th.   No. 8.   J. Duncan Hamilton and P. Fotheringham Parker (Maserati) 49 laps.   Time : 1 hr. 56 mins. 14.8 secs.

Fastest Lap :   Car No. 6.   D. Hampshire (Maserati) lap 18.   Time : 2 mins. 2 secs.   Speed : 94.43 m.p.h.

Apart from its punctured float, the car was as sound as when it started and we had just achieved our aim to be the first unblown car to finish, with a margin of one second, and had learnt a tremendous amount in the process. Our stop for fuel, in which we put in five gallons, took 25 seconds against Whitehead's 20 seconds and Parnell's 32 seconds, although they obviously had to put in more than we, so we felt that, for beginners, we had not done too badly.

It had been our first visit to Jersey and we resolved that it would certainly not be our last, for the Jersey Race really has an atmosphere of its own, very largely due to the ability of the Jersey Club and the B.A.R.C. to run the event with great efficiency and a minimum of red tape and also to the tremendous charm and hospitality of the Jersey people themselves.

On the finance side, we had, of course, been lucky in that the car had stayed in one piece although, even so, the event had cost us more than the whole of our season with the Healey to date. In round figures, the Jersey Race with the H.W.M.

cost us £100, this figure being subdivided as follows : Cost of
fares for ourselves and mechanic and cost of shipping racing
car and van return, £60 ; the balance of £40 being made up
by our own and mechanic's hotel accommodation, mechanic's
time, and incidentals.

Even so, it had been a great experience, from my point of
view, to have handled one of these cars in a race of this size,
and had it not been for my partner's kindness I should certainly not have been able to do so.   Loath as we were to leave
Jersey, we had to get back to our responsibilities at home, and
we left Jersey airport promptly at eight next morning, arriving
home at Weybridge at ten, via Northolt, the H.W.M. and
its van crossing back by boat next day.

CHAPTER V

At Silverstone

BEFORE we left for Jersey I had left the Healey with Messrs. Thomson and Taylor at Brooklands for, although the car was running as well as it had on the day we bought it, we had done nothing to it whatever apart from regular greasing and routine maintenance and as we had only got one more Goodwood Meeting before the Production Car Race at Silverstone and the T.T. in Ireland, I thought that in view of the enormous amount of work it had done, the time had come when we really ought to give it something in the nature of an overhaul.

As regards the chassis, transmission and engine, it was not easy to decide what was to be done because the car had never missed a beat or given any trouble in this direction since we had had it, but there were one or two body rattles developing and the brakes obviously required some attention which might well amount to relining. We also were in need of some new tyres and, having had them fitted, I left the car with Ken Taylor, world renowned for his contributions to John Cobb's Land Speed Record with the Napier Railton, with instructions to proceed with such work as he thought necessary, bearing in mind the work we had already done and were proposing to do with the car. I fully expected a fairly heavy bill on my return from Jersey and was very delighted to find one for only £3 18 3, which included filling the car with £1 10 8 worth of petrol. Moreover, Ken told me that, having tried the car, they thought that it was going so well from the mechanical angle that, unless I particularly wanted the engine stripped, they were loath to disturb it. Needless to say I completely agreed, and so our overhaul was confined to the body, brakes and exhaust system which had been found to be in need of attention.

I collected the car from Thomson and Taylor the day before

the Goodwood Club Meeting on August 12th, some change having taken place in our plans for this meeting for the following reasons. In the first place, since Jean was now driving so well, and since I had had such an unexpectedly large slice of driving at Jersey, we agreed that she should run the Healey in both a scratch race and a handicap at Goodwood while I should drive it in a handicap only. Now, however, another development cropped up, for " Buster " Baring had sold the H.W.M. and had ordered in its place a new Frazer-Nash Le Mans Replica which he hoped to have in time for the Production Car Race at Silverstone on August 26th. As the car would obviously not be ready for the Goodwood Meeting on the 12th, Jean and I had suggested to " Buster " that he should drive the Healey in my place at that meeting and this he agreed to do.

Accordingly, therefore, we all met at Goodwood on the 12th, where the faithful Healey once more prepared for battle on its home ground. Both Jean and " Buster " did about ten practice laps each without incident and we then put the car away in its paddock stall in readiness for its first race which was the five-lap scratch race for cars up to 3 litre, in which, of course, Jean was to drive. There was a formidable entry for this race, the highlights being Anthony Crook's Le Mans Frazer-Nash, Kenneth McAlpine's Connaught, R. F. Peacock's Frazer-Nash B.M.W., B. A. Chevell's Alvis and Robin Richards' and B. Webb Ware's Silverstone Healeys, the latter car being driven by P. de F. C. Pycroft.

We had compared notes previously with Robin Richards and knew that our car was quite a bit faster than his although we knew little about the light green car that Pycroft was driving, although we had noticed it being particularly well driven by him at one of the Goodwood official practice days earlier on in the season.

The field for this race was a fairly large one and when the ballot was announced, we found that we had been unlucky and had drawn a third row starting position. In case it may be helpful I will explain a little trick that we adopted in cases where we were unlucky enough to draw starting positions other than in the front row.

As soon as the result of the ballot is announced, competitors can usually get a copy of it, showing the racing numbers of the cars in their respective rows. In this case the starting positions were as follows :—

First Row	..	44	42	36		38
Second Row	..		32	34	35	
Third Row	..	43	45	41		39
Fourth Row	..			48	33	

From this it can be seen that there are four cars in the front row, three in the second, four in the third and two in the fourth. Underlining our own number, we would then strike out all those cars we felt fairly sure of beating at the start, leaving in the ones which we thought would be likely to beat us. Applying the scheme to this particular race we deduced as follows :—

In the first row, we felt able to cope with all except car number 42, which was McAlpine's Connaught, so we struck out car numbers 44, 36 and 38. In row two we left car number 32 and struck out car numbers 34 and 35, car number 32 being Peacock's Frazer-Nash B.M.W. In row three we left car number 43, R. C. Willis' Frazer-Nash B.M.W., struck out cars 41 and 39 and underlined our own number 45, and in the last row we struck out car number 33 and left in number 48, Anthony Crook's Frazer-Nash.

The picture one now gets therefore is :—

First Row	..	—	42	—	—
Second Row	..	32	—	—	
Third Row	..	43	45	—	—
Fourth Row	..		48	—	

Now one can see at a glance where the potential menaces are situated and in this particular race it can be seen that they are all grouped towards the near or left-hand side of the track. Obviously, in this case, we should aim to take a wide course into the right-hand curve at Madgwick Corner as by doing so we should be more likely to be in the company of cars going faster rather than slower than our own. In this case, I anticipated McAlpine going off like a rocket before any of his real rivals could get clear of the crush, although I thought that Peacock, in the second row, would not be far behind.   Willis, in our own row would, I knew, make a terrific start although I personally didn't regard the lasting capabilities of his car tremendously highly.   Our own car, I felt, was completely the reverse to Willis' being not too brisk off the mark, but 100 per cent. reliable while, in the back row, Anthony Crook was obviously McAlpine's closest rival if he were ever able to disentangle himself from the field in time to get within striking distance.

This scheme, of course, has its drawbacks, for cars are notoriously temperamental, and seldom perform as anticipated, while one quite small misjudgment by a driver in a forward row can easily transform the whole picture, but it was a scheme that we adopted at the beginning of the season when Jean didn't know all her rivals personally and we found it well worth continuing throughout the season.

In this case it did not really work because Peacock was unable to make his usual excellent get away and when they came round at the end of the first lap, McAlpine had got completely clear while all his other rivals were still well entangled, although Anthony Crook was coming through the field quickly.   Jean had got ahead of Peacock who was in the process of passing her as they came by me.   The position remained the same until the third lap when the order was : McAlpine, Peacock, Crook, Pycroft, with our own car in fifth place, but this was the decisive lap, for Crook retired at the end of it with some trouble not specified, while Jean was able to get by Pycroft who was going great guns in Webb Ware's Healey.   From then on the positions never altered, and McAlpine came in the winner, followed by Peacock who had had a rather hectic drive according to all accounts, while Jean was third, with Pycroft an excellent fourth.

This race was the third of the afternoon and we now had a long wait until " Buster " took over in Race 8 and Jean followed with her handicap in Race 9, which was the last of the day.   Crook was the scratch man in " Buster's " race while Willis received 22 secs. start from him and we received 28 secs. and had to give 5 secs. start to Pycroft and no less than 25 secs. to Philip Fotheringham Parker's supercharged " 2.3 " Alfa-Romeo. The field was a fairly small one and we felt that these were the cars most likely to make the running. We were fairly confident in being able to cope with poor Crook on these terms, but we were not happy about Willis, although he was a doubtful starter, having had trouble in the scratch race earlier in the afternoon. We weren't sure about Pycroft who was going very well indeed and we hoped to cope with Philip and his Alfa despite its handicap, for it had not sounded too healthy in practice.

Here, again, our calculations only proved partially right, for although he was able to fend off the Frazer-Nash, " Buster " was held up by a slower car while in pursuit of Pycroft, while Philip had got his 2.3 Alfa really motoring and won the race in fine style followed by Pycroft with our own car again in third place.

A remarkable thing at these meetings and, for that matter, at all the meetings we had attended so far, was our inability to win a race either on scratch or on handicap. We had hardly run at one meeting without getting a second or third place but, with the exception of the first outing, we had had with the car we had never had an outright win, however small. To offset this, of course, we had never yet failed to finish a race and we felt that this perhaps made up for our inability to achieve outright wins.

At the completion of his race, " Buster " rushed the car to the starting paddock for Jean to take over in her handicap race and here she had a really Herculean task, for out of the goodness of his heart, the handicapper had given her, the only girl in the race, a scratch start in a race full of men. She had to concede 2 mins. to the joint limit men M. G. Thomas and E. E. Sears on M.G.s and was on the line for no less than 25 secs. by herself after D. C. Hull and M. H. Buckler her nearest neighbours had left.

Despite this, her chances of getting a place did not seem to me hopeless provided she had some luck in getting through the field when she began to catch them during the later stages of the race. Unfortunately, however, we were again unlucky in this respect, for the field became very bunched indeed

towards the third of the five laps and she was slowed right
down to the speed of some of the slower cars in lap four
although she ultimately managed to procure fifth place at the
finish. We had considerable consolation though, for during
the course of the race Jean broke her own ladies' lap record
by putting in a lap at 1 min. 53.8 secs., equivalent to a speed of
76.10 miles an hour. This was officially quoted as the third
fastest lap of the day and was only beaten by Anthony Crook
on his Frazer-Nash and by Guy Gale on the big Darracq in
the scratch race for cars over three litres in capacity. It was
also well over a second faster than I myself had ever done with
the car at Goodwood and was, of course, easily the fastest lap
ever put up officially by a Healey at Goodwood to date. This
went a long way to consoling her for having been unable to get
a place in the race and provided a high note for the finish of
her 1950 racing season at Goodwood, ladies not being eligible
to compete at the Autumn Meeting in September.

We now began to prepare for our first long race with the
car, the Production Car Race at the meeting sponsored by the
Daily Express at Silverstone and being run for them by the
British Racing Drivers' Club. The *Daily Express* had already
done British Motor Sport a tremendous amount of good by
sponsoring this meeting in 1949 when it had been an enormous
success and it was to be run again on very similar lines in 1950.

The main event was, of course, the International *Daily
Express* Trophy Race for Formula 1 cars which had attracted
a representative entry from France, Italy, Belgium and Great
Britain, and although the cream of the Continental drivers
were taking part, including the so far unbeaten Alfa-Romeo
cars, two of which were to be driven by Guiseppe Farina and
Juan Manuel Fangio, the big attraction here was the new
National British Racing Car the B.R.M., which was appearing
for the first time ever and which was to be driven by the
world-famous driver Raymond Sommer.

Supporting the main event was the Production Car Race
which, as its name implies was a race for cars in series production and which could be bought by the public. This had
received such a tremendous entry that it had been split into
two sections, which were again subdivided into classes respectively. The first section included all cars having a capacity

of up to 2 litres and included classes for cars of 1,100-c.c., 1,500-c.c. and 2 litres, while the second section, which was scheduled to be run off later in the day, was for cars of over 2 litres and was subdivided into classes for cars of over 2 but under 3 litres and again, over 3 litres. As our Healey's capacity was 2,443-c.c. it came in the 3-litre class, running at the same time as the big cars in the afternoon.

In addition to these events there was a ten-lap race for 500-c.c. cars and last but not least, a parade of historic racing cars showing the progress in design throughout the years.

As enormous crowds were expected at Silverstone, to which access had been very difficult at past meetings, we decided to stay at Oxford on Thursday and Friday nights, August 24th and 25th, and we booked accommodation at the Randolph Hotel.

The entry for our section of the Production Car Race was made up of five Jaguar X.K.120 two-seaters, to be driven by Tony Rolt, Peter Walker, Leslie Johnson, Tommy Wisdom and A. J. C. Schwelm ; four Allards, the drivers being S. H. Allard, Cuthbert Harrison, K. Watkins and F. G. Curtis ; three of the lovely Aston Martin Aerodynamic Coupés to be driven by Reg Parnell, Lance Macklin and Eric Thomson ; two Lea-Francis, a saloon to be driven by F. R. G. Spikins, and a sports tourer, the driver of which was K. H. F. Rose. Then there was a Riley saloon to be driven by G. H. Grace, an Alfa-Romeo by S. J. Gilbey, an Austin A.90 by Ken Wharton, a Healey saloon by K. H. Downing and no less than eight Healey Silverstones, the drivers being Robin Richards, Guy Gale, Leslie Onslow Bartlett, Sir Francis Samuelson, David Lewis, W. Freed, Duncan Hamilton and myself. Of these, it later transpired that Lewis' car was in fact Onslow Bartlett's and had been purchased from him shortly before the race, while the car to be driven by Duncan Hamilton was entered and prepared by the works themselves. This we regarded as a very special menace and we knew also that Guy Gale's car had had attention from no less a person than Freddie Dixon himself. The other Healeys we had run against previously and had come out on top, although we thought it very likely that some of them now had considerably more steam than they had had earlier on in the season.

The race was one of particular interest for us because, in the first place, we had accepted an invitation from Guy Gale to run in a team with himself and Robin Richards. There was, of course, a team prize to be won and our entry was put in by Automobilia Ltd., a garage of which Guy was a director, at Dorking. Another point of great interest was the works car which Duncan was driving, for this, we were told, was fitted with high compression pistons which, so far, we had not used in our car. There was, of course, no reason why we should not have used these had we wished to do so, but we were not absolutely sure whether they would not prove too high for the fuel supplied for the race by the organizers, and for this reason alone we decided to continue with the same set of pistons we had used throughout the season.

At the last moment there was a great sensation, for it was announced that yet another Jaguar X.K.120 would be driven by the world-famous Italian driver Tazio Nuvolari, who was to arrive in time to practise with the car at the first session on Thursday the 24th.

The race had its personal problems for us because our young son's nanny was due to have her holiday at that time and for a while we couldn't see how we were going to find a solution to this problem which would have meant that Jean could not have given her usual help to our *équipe*. Hearing of our troubles, my mother-in-law kindly offered to take over young Charles, although we resolved to ease the burden slightly by my going up to Silverstone alone on Thursday morning in the Healey, while Jean and my sister-in-law Anne followed in the Citroën, meeting me at the Randolph Hotel in Oxford, on Thursday evening.

Arriving at Silverstone, I found the usual feverish preparation in progress everywhere, my team mate Robin Richards being in the throes of fitting shock absorbers to his car, while Guy Gale had not yet arrived from Dorking. Duncan was ready, however, and we decided to go out to practise together, I being grateful of an opportunity to follow someone who knew the circuit on which I had not driven before, while both of us were interested to see how our respective cars compared for speed.

With the exception of Guy Gale, Sir Francis Samuelson, Wharton, Gilbey, Freed and Schwelm, the entire field for this race had turned out for practice, Nuvolari's car being beautifully finished in red, the Italian racing colours. For the first few practice laps, Duncan led and I followed, gradually memorizing each bend and noting carefully his braking points and approaches. After five or six laps we came in for a routine check over and it was agreed that I should now lead and should gradually work up to as high a speed as possible.

As I had not got Jean as timekeeper, I prevailed on an old friend of mine, Guy Templar, to perform this function for me and most capably he did it. On the face of it it does not appear a very difficult job, provided one has got two stop watches, to time one car on every lap, but it is amazingly hard to find someone able to do it accurately. The principal difficulty is that an inexperienced timekeeper's attention is so easily distracted by the numerous happenings around him that his mind easily wanders and he misses the car he is timing. There is nothing more galling from a driver's point of view to be told on coming in, " I missed one or two laps, but I think they would have been quite as good or perhaps better than the ones I have got." To my mind there is only one thing worse, and that is for a timekeeper to guess at a lap time he has missed and to quote it to the driver as authentic. This, I think, is quite unforgivable, for it leads everyone up the garden, particularly if it errs on the side of optimism, which it usually does. To be told that one's time has been missed is annoying, involving as it does a certain amount of wasted effort, but the situation can be put right by further practice.

Guy Templar was, I knew, completely reliable, having had a wealth of experience at Brooklands and elsewhere before the war and I was very lucky to be able to " Press Gang " him into acting for me in Jean's absence. At the conclusion of our first six laps he gave our best lap as 2 mins. 18 secs., which meant an average of 75.36 m.p.h., and which seemed fairly good to me, bearing in mind my limited knowledge of the circuit. We then went out again, I leading, and began to try hard to whittle down the time lap by lap. After another five laps I began to feel much happier, particularly because we seemed to be passing quite a lot of people while nobody had so far passed us. Try as I would, however, I could not shake Duncan off. He remained tightly on my tail and, thinking that I might be holding him up, I waved him by and continued to follow him as before. He didn't appear to be able to get far away, though, and a few laps later we were both highly gratified to find ourselves passing first Nuvolari on the Jaguar, and later, Reg Parnell on one of the Aston Martins.

All too soon, our practice period ended and we went together to the Clerk of the Course's office to obtain a copy of all the official practice times so far recorded. According to Guy Templar's reckoning, we had got down to 2 mins. 11 secs. dead, which was equivalent to 79.38 m.p.h., a speed which he thought had been only bettered by the Jaguars. I must confess that we found this hard to believe, but when the official times were announced, we found that he was absolutely right and that we had, in fact, put up equal third best practice time.

The exact speeds were as follows : Tony Rolt and Peter Walker both on Jaguars, 81.24 m.p.h. ; Duncan and myself, 79.38 m.p.h. ; Leslie Johnson (Jaguar), 78.19 m.p.h. ; Reg Parnell (Aston Martin), 77.61 ; Eric Thompson (Aston Martin), 77.03 ; Tazio Nuvolari and Tommy Wisdom (Jaguars), 75.91 m.p.h. ; Cuthbert Harrison (Allard), 77.61 ; and so on down to Spikins' Lea-Francis saloon which had done 66 m.p.h.

Although I realized that these were the first day's times and were therefore almost certain to be improved upon on the following day, I was really pleased and extremely grateful to Duncan, without whose help I knew that I must have been much slower. My driving lacked and would, I felt, always lack his zest and if I had had my way I would have put the car away then and there and not taken it out again until the day of the race. Not so Duncan ; not only was he going to practise again on the following day, but he was insistent that I should do the same. He felt sure, he said, that we could improve on these speeds, and try we must.

Although I felt far from sure, I agreed to turn out and we

left the circuit with a definite date for the morrow. I now knew that for the first time throughout the season I had come upon a Healey Silverstone that was quite a bit faster than our own and piloted by a faster driver into the bargain. Nevertheless, I refused to be too downcast, for although I knew that both Duncan and his car were faster, I remembered that he had not always been entirely consistent in the past and I secretly hoped, without wishing him any ill will, that he might repeat his " spin round " at Jersey if I could get near enough to press him.

As I drove back to Oxford that evening in the Healey I couldn't help marvelling at the old car's record, for the clock had now done a complete revolution and she was back at Silverstone practising again for the same race as the one with which she had begun her career a year ago. Moreover, she had done a season's racing without having had so much as a decoke and was now performing as creditably as when she was new. In a way, I wished that I had had the higher pistons fitted, but we had been trying to keep expense down and I thought that, after all, I had probably done the right thing.

On arrival at the Randolph I found that Jean and Anne had just beaten me to it and having bathed and changed we enjoyed a really first-class dinner over which we made our plans for the morrow. We found that our presence was not required at Silverstone until after lunch and, as we anticipated a really long and hectic day on the Saturday, we decided to treat ourselves to a late morning on Friday. We breakfasted at nine, therefore, and then made a tour of the shops in Oxford, arriving at Silverstone between one and two and in good time to have the car scrutineered before continuing practice. The scrutineering, always rather more comprehensive for a race of this size than for a normal club event, produced no real headaches although there was some discussion as to the best way of officially sealing the fuel and radiator caps.

Both my team mates, Robin and Guy, were going to practise, and although Samuelson's and Freed's Healeys were also there, together with Gilbey's Alfa-Romeo, there was still no sign of Schwelm's Jaguar or Wharton's Austin, and these cars, not having practised the day before, would not, of course, be able to run unless they put in an appearance to-day. The same, by the way, was being said about the B.R.M., which to everyone's surprise had not arrived to date, although we were assured that it would turn up later in the day and that all was quite well.

No sooner had we completed our scrutineering session than the circuit was open and once again, accompanied this time by Guy Gale and Robin, I joined battle with Duncan. His car had been back to the works and had had some attention to the brakes and suspension since the previous day and it had evidently paid a dividend for, whereas I had been just able to keep up with him yesterday, I now found that I could definitely not hold him, try as I would.

I had done about five laps when I suddenly noticed, to my horror, that the oil pressure was dropping as I came out of Stowe Corner and watching carefully, I found that the same was happening at Club Corner, except that this time it dropped nearly to zero. The trouble, as it was happening on fast bends, was obviously oil surge and I immediately pulled into the pits to check the level. Finding it to be slightly below maximum, I filled it to slightly above maximum in order to make quite sure of curing the trouble, and then set out again to see the effect.

The effect was not quite what I had expected for, although I had cured the surge and the oil pressure now remained constant, I now found that I had, in my ignorance, brought on another trouble by overfilling the sump. Alongside the filler on the sump of the Riley engine in the Healey is a pipe which allows oil to drain from the sump when it is filled above its proper level and as the car rounded the right-hand bends on the circuit, surplus oil drained from the level pipe on to the exhaust pipe so much so that the marshal at Club Corner reported that the car appeared to be on fire as it rounded the corner.

This brought Earl Howe to our pit to advise us of the report and to investigate its cause although by the time he arrived we had discovered the error and rectified it. I then went out again for a final few laps during which, according to Jean, I clipped one second off my previous day's best lap so that now

[*Photos : D. G. Collins*

*" We scuttle across
the concrete "*

" We're away "

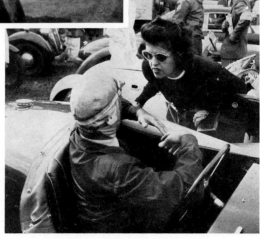

*"Why . . . I had been
so slow."*

B.R.O.C. PRODUCTION CAR RACE, SILVERSTONE, AUGUST, 1950

[Photo : F.J. Brymer

" On her first run Mrs. Stapleton had plug trouble "

BRIGHTON SPEED TRIALS SEPTEMBER 1950

I had lapped the circuit in 2 mins. 10 secs., which equalled a speed of 79.99 m.p.h., although, as I had anticipated, Duncan had pipped me by yet another second, getting round at 80.61 m.p.h.

Much to our surprise, Nuvolari had not turned out again with the Jaguar due to illness and his place had been filled by Peter Whitehead. Lance Macklin, also, was not driving as he had a poisoned hand and his place had been taken by Raymond Sommer who had come over specially to drive the B.R.M., which incidentally, had still not appeared at the end of the second and final day's practice. Gilbey's Alfa-Romeo had been slow on both the straights and on the bends, his best lap being given officially as 2 mins. 59 secs., which was not even fast enough to show on the official speed table which began at a lap speed of 2 mins. 53 secs., equalling a speed of 60.11 m.p.h.

When the official speeds had been announced we found that although we had managed to improve slightly on our previous day's times, others had, as we had expected, improved even more and the bill was topped now by Cuthbert Harrison who had taken the big Allard round at 85.24 m.p.h. Tony Rolt and Peter Walker had tied again with 83.19 m.p.h., then came Sommer on Macklin's Aston Martin at 81.24 m.p.h., followed by Duncan and the works Healey together with Reg Parnell (Aston Martin) and Whitehead (Jaguar) at 80.61 m.p.h. I came next at 79.99 m.p.h., followed by Curtis' Allard at 79.38 m.p.h., then came Wisdom's Jaguar and Guy Gale's Healey at 78.78 m.p.h.

I now knew, beyond all doubt, that I could not possibly cope with Duncan and the works Healey or the Aston Martins, although I had expected there would be an even greater margin between the Healeys and the Aston Martins which were reputed to have a maximum speed far in excess of our cars. I was surprised also that our times had been so close to the Jaguars and the Allards, for we were giving away a litre to the former and no less than 3 litres to the biggest Allard, which was being driven by Harrison instead of by its nominated driver, G. Warburton.

Compared with these times, Ferrari and Frazer-Nash had

G

stood out in the up to 2-litre category, Ascari leading with 84.45 m.p.h., followed by Bob Gerard and Anthony Crook with 82.53 and 80.61 m.p.h. respectively. Oddly enough, Chinetti on the second Ferrari had been very much slower, his best official practice lap being put in at only 72.72 m.p.h., this car being taken over for the race by Serafini.

All seemed set for the race on the day following, but as we knew that there would be tremendous crowds, and possibly a repetition of the fearful traffic jam when the Grand Prix of Europe had been held at Silverstone earlier in the season, we decided to leave the car inside the circuit so that if the traffic approaching the track became absolutely solid, we could at least hitch hike our way there, content in the knowledge that the Healey was already safely there, so having completed all the necessary formalities such as the final sealing of oil, water and fuel fillers, we again made our way back to Oxford, this time in the Citroën.

We had been assured by all the experts that as new traffic arrangements were being put into force, there would be no repetition of the May traffic jam, but we decided to take no chances, particularly as the first race was being started at 10.30 a.m. We planned, therefore, to leave Oxford at 7.30 a.m. at the latest and went to bed early on Friday night leaving strict instructions to be called at 6 a.m. promptly on Saturday morning. I wondered, even so, during the night whether we had planned to leave early enough, for from two in the morning onwards, traffic began to roll past our bedroom *en route* for the circuit.

As the day dawned we saw that it was far from ideal, for it had rained heavily during the night and was still drizzling slightly, but by the time we left for Silverstone it had stopped raining and the sun was trying hard to break through. The traffic appeared to have slowed down slightly and as we made our way out on to the Bicester road we only saw about a dozen or so cars all told. The same applied between Bicester and Buckingham, and as we pulled into Buckingham we began to think that the thing really was under control after all. How wrong we were, for on reaching the centre of the town, we came upon it !

The thing that struck us as we came upon the jam was the

attitude of complete resignation of everyone there.   Engines
were stopped, and had been stopped for the past quarter of
an hour, the queue not having moved during that time.   Parties
were breakfasting to the accompaniment of radios, nobody
seemed to mind and nobody seemed to have expected anything else.   We waited for five—ten—fifteen minutes during
which time we moved about thirty yards and deciding that we
should never make it unless we adopted really drastic measures,
we took the bull by the horns and, sticking all our " Competitor " and " Competitor's Tender " placards on the wind-
screen and our " Driver " and " Pit Attendant " brassards on
our arms, we went into action in the offside stream.

We were lucky in not meeting one vehicle coming in the
opposite direction between Buckingham and the circuit itself
and the co-operation and encouragement we received from all
in the nearside stream would have had to have been seen to be
believed.   For the entire way we received nothing but assistance from enthusiasts who told us, in some cases, that they
had moved a hundred and fifty yards in the last hour.   As we
got nearer the circuit, the nearside stream did begin to move
spasmodically, so we moved back into it, finally arriving in
the paddock just after 9.15.   Already, the public enclosures
presented a fantastic sight, for they appeared, at this early
hour, to be packed to capacity and how our unfortunate
friends, still making their way from Buckingham were going to
get in, we couldn't imagine.

The regrettable story of the B.R.M. has been told and retold
so many times that there is little point in my adding to the
volume of opinions already expressed, but it was, by now,
common knowledge that the car was in great trouble, for it
had again failed to appear for practice the previous day.   But
it appeared to take advantage of a special practice period
allotted to it, completing three laps at slightly over 80 m.p.h.
on the very wet circuit.   The car looked and sounded magnificent and it was a thousand pities that it should have failed
so lamentably in its first race later on that afternoon.   Finance
figures of £200,000 were mentioned in connection with the car
in that day's newspapers and still, it was said, the Trust was
short of money. Every car, one knows, has its teething troubles
but, comparing the mournful history of the B.R.M. with the

magnificent results achieved by John Heath with his team of 2-litre (Formula 2) H.W.M.s with no financial assistance from anyone I, in common with most others, could not understand it. The contrast was emphasized even more strongly by the terrific performance of the H.W.M.s driven by Stirling Moss and Fergus Anderson against Formula 1 opposition at this meeting and yet John was marketing these little cars at an approximate figure of £2,500 apiece !

No sooner, it seemed, had we arrived at the circuit, seen the B.R.M. do its qualifying laps and watched the ten-lap race for 500-c.c. cars run off, than it was 11 a.m. and the up to 2-litre Production Car Race was about to begin.   I was very anxious indeed to watch the start of this from the pits, for the method of starting was one which I had never so far tried or even seen, for these races had what were known as Le Mans type starts. Instead of the drivers sitting in their cars with engines running at the start, the cars were parked at one side of the track, in herringbone formation with engines dead, while the drivers were lined up along the other side of the track, having to sprint to their cars, start the engines and close the doors before getting away.

It was impressed upon us that under no circumstances must we get into our cars in any other way than by opening the doors and that the doors must be closed before the car moved off.   I decided to watch the start of this race from behind Bob Gerard's pit, feeling sure that Bob would waste no time at all in getting started and thereby got a good idea of just how the job should be done.   There had been a certain amount of leg pulling at my expense in our *équipe*, Jean maintaining that I was far too stout and well nourished to run fast and that I should have to drive the car all the faster by virtue of the time I should lose at the start.   She was supported, I suspected, by my sister-in-law, Anne, who, although she said nothing, tacitly agreed, I felt sure, with Jean.   I resolved, therefore, to put my best foot forward when my turn came, although after watching the start of the up to 2-litre race, I felt none too confident.

As had been expected, the two Ferraris driven by Ascari and Serafini dominated the race throughout, although the Frazer-Nashs gave them a good run for their money, Newton's car eventually finishing third. Then followed the two heats of the Formula 1 race, Farina winning the first in his Alfa-Romeo at 90.01 m.p.h. and Fangio, similarly mounted, winning the second in pouring rain at 76.73 m.p.h. While the first heat was comparatively devoid of incident, the second will probably stick in the minds of many for the tragic failure of the B.R.M. actually on the starting line, but even more for the fantastic driving by Brian Shawe Taylor in finishing an excellent second to Fangio, driving, as usual, his veteran B type E.R.A. Shawe Taylor, always at his best in the rain, gave an exhibition of driving under really bad conditions, that went a long way towards compensating most people for the B.R.M. debacle.

By the time this heat finished we were all ready for the start of our race and although the rain had stopped by now, the circuit was still really slippery as we went round on our preliminary warming up lap. At the conclusion of this, we lined the cars up diagonally by the pits alongside the course and no sooner had we done so than the siren was blowing and at the same time the board was being displayed showing that there was now an interval of only five minutes to go before the start.

We took up our places on the other side of the course, and the minutes ticked away relentlessly. Four minutes, three, two, and I began to wonder whether the old car would start as perfectly as she always had. I looked across to the pit to find that my staff were already in fits of laughter. The joke about my not being able to run had by now grown whiskers until someone had suggested that if I really ran as slowly as was alleged, I ought to be careful not to get run over by other drivers who had got into their cars and were away before I had even reached mine. I looked at Duncan who was next door and who was still sitting on a straw bale nonchalently watching the starter. I wondered ; would the car start, would it start ? Someone in an M.G. had failed to get away at once in the up to 2-litre race and had been left madly winding the handle. Would the same thing happen to me ? Why I should have thought so I can't imagine, because of all the cars I have ever owned, the Healey was the best starter ever. But on every other occasion it hadn't mattered particularly whether it started first push of the button or not. This time every-thing depended on it. Suddenly I heard the announcer on the loud speaker. " Twenty seconds to go." My feet felt as though they were filled with lead and as I looked down the line I thought, " How ridiculous we look." Fat men, thin men, men wearing visors, men wearing goggles, boxing boots, plimsolls, queer shirts, as incongruous a collection as one would meet anywhere. And now we were going to run ! It seemed fantastic !

Then suddenly : " Ten seconds to go." I put my goggles down. " Five, four, three, two, one " and down goes the flag and we scuttle across the concrete as though our very lives depend on it. At last—the car—open the door—hurl myself in—left hand switch on—right hand slam door—left hand engage first gear—right hand press starter.

Dead silence all along the line—but no, No—the engine's running. A fraction of a second to build up some revs. and we're away before Duncan or Guy Gale on either side have moved. As we gather way, the entire line, it seems, get going and we roar down to Woodcote Corner right on the tail of the three Aston Martins driven by Sommer, Reg Parnell and Eric Thompson. Suddenly I realize that there is a car along-side trying desperately to get through and out of the corner of my eye I recognize Duncan—very determined, grimly deter-mined, in fact, and obviously in no mood to argue. Well, he can have it, as far as I am concerned. It's early yet, and I'd rather see whether the circuit had dried out at all, although I haven't any objection to hanging on to his tail. Copse Corner and the pace is much hotter than I expected under these conditions—Maggots Corner, still very slippery, and as we round Becketts—it happens.

Quite what happened I've never been able to recall accurately. It was very wet and I think the thing started as a tail slide. It finished, however, as a glorious dyed-in-the-wool four-wheel slide, quite out of control with no steering way and no object in braking because the car was going sideways anyhow. I had a glimpse of the grass verge roaring up at terrific speed and had quite decided that the car was going to roll when—to my amazement—I found that I was still motoring albeit with only two wheels still on the track. Obviously, though, the crisis was over and now was the time to accelerate and rejoin the contest. The rest of the lap is completed, I am afraid, at greatly reduced speed and if ever I had any doubts regarding my ability to become a racing driver, I have them now. So far from being the legendary character with nerves of steel and muscles like iron bands I find that, in Healey Number Six there sits an individual with nerves like a juke box and muscles of jelly, an individual who has well and truly frightened himself although he has probably become the wiser in consequence.

As I approach Stowe, I am aware of another car alongside and as we pull away from the corner together, I take a look— and am duly shocked for I find that it is G. H. Grace's $2\frac{1}{2}$-litre Riley full four-seater saloon. Worse is to follow, for it takes me over a lap to get ahead of him and another lap before I really feel that he is shaken off. After five laps, we become fairly well strung out ; there is a blue Allard ahead which seems to be gaining slightly although steadily, and in the mirror I see my team mate Guy Gale in his dark green Healey. Duncan, of course, has vanished into the blue, and by now the circuit has really dried out with the exception of one or two bad patches which are easily remembered and which present no real difficulty.

The race has now become comparatively dull, for we are cracking along without seeing anyone. Guy is gradually falling astern, the Allard has now disappeared from view and for several laps I am motoring entirely alone with no one else in sight at all. I begin to wonder about the progress of the race. We had agreed that unless some very great crisis arose I would not expect to receive any pit signals, for we felt that the race was not long enough to warrant any and that we could more or less foresee the result anyway. I knew that the Jaguars and the big Allard would be way out in front and that the three Aston Martins and Duncan would be filling the first four places in the up to 3-litre class, although I was not sure that there were no other 3-litre cars ahead of me.

Normally, I would have felt fairly sure of the position, for it is not too difficult at the start of a race to see who has gone on ahead, but when I had trouble at Becketts on the first lap,

I was dimly aware that a number of people had gone by without my knowing who they were. I had subsequently passed both David Lewis' and W. Freed's Healeys who had obviously slipped by but could not recall having seen anything of either Sir Francis Samuelson or my other team mate Robin Richards.

I wondered what my pit staff were thinking, for the start really had been a good one although my position in the race at the end of lap one must have been a complete mystery to them. The car was now going perfectly and I felt much more comfortable and had really settled down and was beginning to enjoy myself. I was now expecting to be lapped by the outright leader of the race, and sure enough at the end of lap 13 I discerned in the mirror the form of a green Jaguar which, as it passed, turned out to be driven by Peter Walker, closely followed by Tony Rolt on another Jaguar.

Although I didn't know it at the time, my lap times were steadily improving throughout the race and I now began to lap some of the steadier runners in the race. There were several incidents, one of them, at Maggots Corner, involving Peter Whitehead's Jaguar to no small degree. I found that it was not easy to see exactly what had happened because as I came round for the first time I must have been closely on the tail of the incident, for the marshals on the spot had not yet had time to sort out the correct flags. What I did see, however, caused me not to allow my attention to wander for, out of the corner of my eye, I spotted one marshal hastily grabbing the flag denoting oil on the track.

I wondered whether he'd grabbed it by mistake, but almost at the same moment I felt sure he was right for, on the opposite side of the track, there was apparently a large hole in the fence through which the tail of a car protruded. No sooner had I had time to take all this in than the Healey gave a lurch and if I had ever had any doubts, I now knew that there was indeed oil on the track. To make it more difficult, the oil patch was right on the apex of the bend, but the marshals on the spot must have dealt with it most capably for it was no worse to cross on the next lap and appeared to get steadily better as the race progressed.

A few laps later, having negotiated it once more without incident, I emerged from Becketts to find David Lewis' light blue Healey facing back to front, its driver obviously waiting until there should be a lull in the activity before turning the car round and continuing. I thought that he was very awkwardly placed and my sympathies were with him, for while he stayed there cars were coming upon him at between 75 and 80 miles an hour, with visibility of about 50 yards. On the other hand, to turn the car, he would need to occupy twice as much width of track and if he were not to be collected by an oncoming car, he would have to be pretty quick in the process. Although I thought that the flagging everywhere was excellent, I did not see a flag on this occasion. I would not like to say that one wasn't given, but I didn't see it myself and coming upon David as I did was a source of embarrassment to us both. It may well have been, of course, that the incident had only just occurred and that there had not, as yet, been sufficient time to flag.

Shortly after this, I saw in my mirror another car coming up astern rather more slowly than the two Jaguars and for several laps I was a bit mystified as to what it was. It turned out to be Sommer's Aston Martin which went by me quite slowly on the straight between Chapel Curve and Stowe Corner. Rather to my surprise, it was not followed by the other two Astons and as it had gone by more slowly than I had expected I made an effort to hang on for as long as possible. We approached Stowe, according to my rev. counter, at between 105 and 107 miles an hour, the Aston's stop lights blinked for a moment and before I had really grasped the situation, we were into the corner, the Aston in the most perfectly controlled four-wheel drift imaginable. I was also conscious of being in a slide although in my wildest dreams I could not claim that it was perfectly controlled, but I did get round and, to my great delight, I came out of the corner still on Sommer's tail. We more or less repeated the performance at Stowe, even appeared to gain slightly at Abbey Curve, went past the pits in line ahead and into Woodcote Corner at a pace I just couldn't quite manage.

As we came out, I estimated that I had lost between 15 and 20 yards and I don't think I lost any more at Copse although

Sommer appeared not to have a worry in the world as he crossed the oil patch at Maggots and here again I appeared to have lost about the same distance on this one bend alone. I was now convinced that there was virtually no difference whatever in acceleration between the two cars although the Aston Martin seemed to have about five miles an hour more maximum. But the point was that there were so very few places on the course where we were reaching maximum and it boiled down therefore to the fact that, as I saw it, ninety per cent. of Sommer's gain over my own car had been obtained by his terrific technique on the bends. I continued the losing battle for a few more laps but was forced to admit that despite all I just couldn't come near to coping.

By now, the race was nearing its end and as Sommer disappeared from view a well-known silhouette appeared in my mirror—Duncan with the works Healey ! So Duncan was ahead of the other two Astons and at that rate was not so very far behind Sommer. He passed me at the approach to Stowe, the car sounding very good and taking the corner very fast indeed although, I thought, not as steadily as the Aston Martin. Duncan was obviously on top of his form, shaking with laughter and sticking his tongue out at me as he passed and I decided again to tail him for a bit if I could. But it seemed to me that he was, if anything, faster everywhere than the Aston and I had the greatest difficulty to stay with him for even half a lap. The acceleration of the car was much better than mine and coupled with Duncan's carefree style of driving was obviously likely to, and did in fact produce the results required, for just before the end of the race he caught and passed Sommer, thereby finishing winner of the 3-litre class.

Almost immediately, it seemed, we were given the chequered flag and, on coming in, I was besieged by my staff as to why, after my good start, I had been so slow in the opening laps. Having furnished the explanations, we all went off to the time-keepers' box to obtain copies of the official results and finishing times which were, after all, rather more encouraging than I had expected. They showed that we had finished fifth in the 3-litre class, the full results and speeds being as follows :—

Up to 3,000-*c.c.* :

	Car No.	Driver	Car	Speed	Completed
1st	7	D. Hamilton	Healey	79.92 m.p.h.	28 laps
2nd	14	R. Sommer	Aston Martin	79.90 ,,	28 ,,
3rd	12	R. Parnell	,, ,,	78.34 ,,	28 ,,
4th	15	E. Thompson	,, ,,	77.28 ,,	27 ,,
5th	6	C. Mortimer	Healey	76.61 ,,	27 ,,
6th	5	G. Gale	,,	73.89 ,,	26 ,,

Over 3,000-*c.c.* :

	Car No.	Driver	Car	Speed	Completed
1st	28	P. D. Walker	Jaguar	81.88 m.p.h.	29 laps
2nd	27	A. P. R. Rolt	,,	81.57 ,,	29 ,,
3rd	20	S. H. Allard	Allard	79.49 ,,	28 ,,
4th	24	T. H. Wisdom	Jaguar	78.18 ,,	28 ,,
5th	26	L. G. Johnson	,,	77.41 ,,	27 ,,
6th	22	K. Watkins	Allard	76.93 ,,	27 ,,

These results were quite a pleasant surprise to me because, not only was the speed better than I had expected, bearing in mind the diversion at the beginning of the race, but also because the three Aston Martins and the winning Healey were works entries, whereas both Guy Gale's and my own car were our own personal property and were in daily domestic use on the road.

Again we had raced with virtually no trouble whatever barring the very mild bout of oil surge in practice which had been very easily cured and had taught us that because a car will run satisfactorily for an indefinite period on a given circuit, one must not assume that it will automatically do so on another circuit. Until we brought the car to this Silverstone circuit we had had no trouble with oil surge at all, purely because no other circuit on which we had raced it to date had had such very fast wide radius bends following closely on one another. In any case, as I was told after the race, modifications were already available to prevent this trouble recurring.

The meeting had proved less expensive than I had anticipated, the whole thing, including fuel to and from the circuit and hotel bill for three of us amounting to less than £20, and this was completely offset by bonus and free issues from various sources, so that in the end we could truthfully say that we had had three days great fun free, gratis and for nothing. Moreover, the Healey was still as happy as ever and we now started to turn our thoughts to our *pièce de résistance*, the R.A.C. T.T. on September 16th.

CHAPTER VI

Now for the T.T.

ANDWICHED in between the Production Car Race at
Silverstone on August 26th and the R.A.C. T.T. on
September 16th, we had one more meeting. The
Brighton Speed Trials on Saturday, September 2nd.

Jean was going to drive the car at Brighton and I was to
be manager, and I am afraid I failed dismally in my duties.
In the first place we were rather busy at the office at that time
and when the entry forms arrived for the Brighton Meeting I
filled in the entry form, putting the car in the Capacity Class
for which it was eligible and quite omitting to notice that as
usual there was a special class for lady drivers.

We had run previously at Brighton and knew that the
sports-car classes were run off in the morning and the racing-
car classes and ladies' class in the afternoon. We were
delayed slightly in getting off on Saturday morning and when
we arrived at Brighton we found that our one class had just
been run off, and there were no second runs. There was no
doubt about it, I had not done a good job and had obviously
lost a lot of stripes in the view of the driver so I set off to seek
audience with the Clerk of the Course to see whether he
would agree to our entry being transferred to the ladies' class
later on in the day.

Much to my relief we were given permission to run, although
it was made clear that we could not rank for an award but a
time would be given for each of our runs. This went a long
way to sweeten the atmosphere between driver and assistant
and after we had had a first-class lunch at the Royal Albion
Hotel, at the start end of the course, harmony was completely
restored.

We had always found, however, that if a day started wrong,
it invariably continued wrong and the next hiatus arose when
the timekeepers were unable to give a time for our first run

as it had apparently been missed. On both her runs Jean had been paired off to run with Mrs. Ernest Stapleton, who was driving her husband's 2-litre Aston Martin, which was the very fast car that used to be owned by the late Jock Horsfall.

On her first run, Mrs. Stapleton had plug trouble and had quite some difficulty in completing the course, but when they came up to the line for their second run the Aston sounded much healthier. As the starting lights changed, both cars got away well, the Healey being slightly in the lead although the Aston was not far behind. The finish must have been one of the best of the day, for the Aston just pipped us by a fraction of a second, although neither car was placed in the final results, Miss Betty Haig winning the class easily in her 1,000-c.c. Cooper, Mrs. Allard being second, driving her husband's Allard, and Mrs. Kennard third on another Healey Silverstone.

Mrs. Kennard's place was particularly interesting to us for so many people seemed to be under the impression that our car was so very much faster than most of the other Healeys and yet here, over a straight distance which formed an ideal test, it was beaten by quite a substantial margin. We, ourselves, could not quite understand it for this was the car that Onslow Bartlett had driven at Blandford and we knew that at that time it was certainly no faster if as fast as our own. Nevertheless, although our Brighton time over the Standing Kilometre was a good deal slower than the time we had recorded at Chelmsford earlier in the season over the same distance, we were both firmly convinced that the car was going perfectly satisfactorily and that both Jean's standing starts were as good as she had ever done.

I had been trying to decide what work to do on the car in preparation for the T.T., but apart from certain small details there appeared to be nothing really requiring attention except the brakes and I decided to leave everything else undisturbed except for thoroughly servicing and greasing the car throughout and relining the brakes at the same time.

By the following Saturday, September 9th, everything was completed and the Healey and the Citroën were loaded up ready for departure to Liverpool early on Monday morning,

September 11th. On Sunday evening we received a phone call from Guy Gale to say that he could not get over to drive in Ireland but that the car was to be driven instead by Mike Oliver of Bugatti and Connaught fame. Guy was taking the car up to Liverpool next day, however, and suggested that we should go up in convoy to which we at once agreed. We had arranged to have our cars alongside the special cargo boat in Liverpool not later than 2 p.m. on Monday so it was agreed that we should leave Weybridge not later than 8 a.m.

After our rough crossing to Jersey we had decided to fly from Liverpool to Belfast and our plane was due to leave Liverpool at midday on Tuesday, arriving in Ireland at about 1.30 p.m. We had had a very kind offer from Ernie Wilkinson, the well-known Belfast Healey driver, to meet our cars and to garage them at Messrs. Leslie Porter Ltd., of Belfast, a highly efficient and enthusiastic motor concern of which he was a director. Needless to say we gratefully accepted his offer and, as it later transpired, we might well have been unable to run in the race had it not been for the keenness and hard work carried out for us by his staff.

My sister-in-law Anne was again going to help us and on Monday morning therefore we all set out for Liverpool, Jean and Anne in the Citroën with all our luggage and spares, Guy and I in our respective Healeys. We had a good run up to Liverpool although poor Jean was suffering from a bad sore throat and felt and looked wretched, but we got to Liverpool on time and deposited the cars on the quay, taking a taxi back to the Adelphi Hotel where we were staying the night.

We had some tea, and having seen Guy off on the train we went to the movies, had a good dinner and retired to bed. A howling gale seemed to be blowing which made us very glad that we hadn't braved the sea crossing.

Next morning poor old Jean's throat was less painful but she had by now developed a first-class cold and had almost completely lost her voice into the bargain. We repacked our things and took the bus to the airport only to be told that there was delay and that the plane would almost certainly not leave before 1 p.m. We had lunch at the airport, took off at one and arrived at our destination at half past two, after touching down in the Isle of Man *en route.*

By the time we had made the eleven-mile bus journey from the airport to Belfast and had got hold of our luggage it was nearly tea time and we made our way to the Grand Central Hotel where we were staying. After tea I went down to the docks to find that the cars had already been collected by Ernie Wilkinson's staff and I made my way round to Leslie Porter's to find that both cars had been shipped without incident and without damage. Everything had been laid on for us and a special department set aside in the works, and in addition to our own car, Guy's, Robin's and C. H. Masters' cars were there and Walter Freed was expected to arrive with his car next day.

There had been some confusion in England as to who should make up the respective teams, but it was now agreed that there should be two teams, the first being Richards, Oliver and Masters ; and the second, Wilkinson, Freed and myself. As the circuit was six or seven miles out of Belfast the rest of the day was given up to unpacking our luggage and equipment and getting settled in generally.

On Wednesday morning, after having reported our presence to the R.A.C. Race Organizers office, Jean, Anne and I took the Citroën up to inspect the course, completing about five or six laps at ordinary cruising speeds. It was much more formidable than I had expected and obviously required the maximum amount of practice in order to produce the best results. I think, perhaps, that I had better quote direct from the organizers' description of the course as given in the Official Programme :—

" The new Tourist Trophy Circuit at Dundrod, County Antrim, is a true road course, excellent in character, with many varied types of bend and varying gradients. The total length measures 7 miles, 732 yards ; it is a right-hand circuit—that is to say it is traversed in a clockwise direction, but in addition to its fourteen right-hand corners, it has seven to the left, varying in severity, which provide a good sense of balance. The start and finish point is located at Rushyhill, on the Glenavy road, about nine miles from Belfast. At the end of the pit area, under the bridge which here gives access to the inside of the circuit, there is a very slight right-hand bend ; from here the road is straight and slightly downhill for over half a mile, and a short timed section is incorporated at this, the fastest part of the course. Some idea of the speeds obtainable can be judged from the fact that Peter Whitehead's Grand Prix Ferrari, winner of the recent Ulster Trophy Race, was timed to cover this section at no less than 134.7 m.p.h. After two fast bends, the course turns right at Leathemstown Corner, where, as at many points on this circuit, there is an excellent escape road. A little farther on comes the nasty right-left-right snake over Leathemstown Bridge which has no hump but possesses a low stone parapet to trap the unwary. Then the road rises steadily to the top of the hill at Tullyrusk cross roads, two miles from the start, passing between white stone pillars and then dropping smartly into a dip, rising again to another peak and thereafter falling steadily to the right-hand corner at Cochranstown.

" On this switchback section the drivers of the faster cars must beware of the unsuspected presence of slower vehicles in the dips, while for them heavy braking will be necessary before Cochranstown, although this is not too severe a bend ; here again there is an escape road. At this point the course begins to enter a wooded section, and the slight rise through one or two gentle curves to Quarterland Corner—the three-mile point—is made along a tree-lined avenue, which in places is bordered by sharp banks where road widening has been carried out. Quarterland is a medium right-hander, shaded by overhanging trees, and is immediately followed by Irelands Corner, more open and to the left.

"From this point the road rises, twisting from right to left and undulating for a total distance of a mile and a half to Wheelers Corner, the highest point on the course ; of the many intermediate curves along this stretch, the most severe is the right-hand one at Budore, but even this can be taken fairly fast. After it comes another cross roads, at Jordans Cross, followed by a steeper rise ; by now the circuit is once more running through open country, and spectators in the public enclosure at Wheelers Corner have a magnificent view of both approach and exit for a considerable distance in either direction.

H

"An open level stretch, though not dead straight, terminates in the banked left-hand corner, known as Tornagrough, with another cross roads at its apex, and the awkwardly curved descent that follows, the bends including one quite severe unnamed long left-hander, falls to the hairpin. This is really acute, and reminiscent of that at Dundonald, on the old Ards Circuit ; brakes will be tested to the utmost, and bottom gear brought into use for the first time since leaving the start. Once past this point, the road once more rises gently through gradual left- and right-hand curves ; after the last of these, it flattens out for Quarry Corner, a seemingly interminable right-hand bend. By now nearly seven miles have been covered, but still the pits are not in sight, there are still one or two final minor bends before the boards appear which give warning of the imminence of the pit area, and thenceforth the road commences to fall again slightly, with one final gentle right-hand curve three hundred yards before the finishing line.

"All round the course, the tarred surface is consistently admirable, and should not become over slippery, even in rain. The average width of the road is at least thirty feet although this varies slightly, there are no abrupt bottle necks, if one excepts the inevitable return to normal width after the pit area itself. Spectators are permitted to line a large portion of the course ; there are excellent enclosures on all the major corners, and grandstands at Quarry and opposite the pits. Altogether the new course at Dundrod is the true road circuit in the best possible tradition, incorporating a wealth of interesting features and many natural hazards, but without any sections involving needless risk, either to competitors or spectators."

From this description it can be seen that, whatever its faults, the course could not be said to be lacking in variety and one look was sufficient to convince us that plenty of practice was absolutely essential. On Wednesday morning, having taken the Citroën round for five or six laps, I went back to Belfast to get the Healey. Although the sun had been shining when we were out in the Citroën it was foggy and raining hard when I got back to the circuit with the Healey an hour later. As I drove up there with sidelights on, the familiar shape of a Jaguar X.K.120, driven by Stirling Moss, loomed up out of the murk on its way back to Belfast, having put in some unofficial lappery.

Arriving back at the circuit, I found that visibility was about fifteen to twenty yards and as it was obviously impossible to learn anything under these conditions, I made my way to the pits where I had some sandwiches while waiting for conditions to improve or worsen.

Half an hour later they appeared to be better and I got in the car and started off slowly. I found at once that the pits side of the course from Wheelers Corner to Rushyhill was having the worst of it and that on the other side, conditions were now quite good.

The roads, of course, were open and it was only possible to cruise fairly fast and to learn the general direction of the various bends, and under these conditions I completed just over a hundred miles, having stopped at some of the trickier places to study them on foot. I felt now that I had a good general idea of the course and that I had certainly saved a lot of valuable official practice time for when the first official practice began, I should at any rate know which way the course went and should be able to try to go fast more or less at once.

As far as the car was concerned, everything appeared to be all right, and having checked it over I took it back to the garage in readiness for the official scrutineering next morning. This, in turn, went off without a hitch, the car's fuel tank being drained and refilled, everything being rigorously checked to ensure that it was exactly as supplied and described in the manufacturer's catalogue. Finally the car was weighed with full tanks, the weight being just under 21-cwt., while it was found that the fuel tank held just over 15 gallons.

By lunch time it had started to rain again and by the time we were up at the pits for practice in the afternoon conditions were again nearly as bad as they had been earlier in the morning. Practice was late in starting, but at last we were off and having completed three laps at semi-racing speed I then started to try to work the speed up bit by bit. The course was proving slightly easier to memorize than I had expected but by now I didn't feel entirely happy about the brakes of the car. Although the pedal had not gone down as I had expected it would, the brakes appeared to need considerable pedal pressure to produce the effects required, particularly on the steep downhill approach to Cochranstown and at the hairpin on the other side of the course.

By the time I had done three more laps I was finding the same everywhere, and they were now so bad that I decided that I could do no more practice until something had been done. That was obviously not possible at the pits; so as far as this practice period was concerned I had had it, and I brought the car into the pits to seek out the brake lining experts in attendance there. All I could do was to make arrangements with Messrs. Leslie Porter to have the drums removed by first thing next morning when it was agreed that the brake lining king would meet me there in order to hold an inquest on the subject.

Although I was disappointed at the great waste of time, I was now more glad than ever that I had spent some time in unofficially running round the course for, had I not done so, I should not now have had time to learn it properly, for practice on the Friday was to be held at 2 p.m. instead of 5 p.m. on the Thursday.

Promptly at nine next morning I made my way round to the garage to find that the technical experts had already beaten me to it and, furthermore, had held their inquest in my absence, deciding that a change of linings was necessary and that they could let me have the brake shoes back, relined and ready to fit in two hours. The snag was that the linings they were proposing to fit required a lot of running before they could be used to the maximum and this meant that it would be after midday before the car would be on the road again while official practice was at 2 p.m. There was nothing to be done about it, however, and I should obviously just have to wait and be ready to rush the car up to the course again as soon as it was available.

I had by now had a look at the official practice times put up the previous evening and found that, as I had expected, my own time was easily the slowest of the Healeys, Robin Richards leading our brigade with a lap of 6 mins. 15 secs., followed by Ernie Wilkinson with 6.18, Masters 6.24, Mike Oliver in Guy Gale's car 6.50, Walter Freed 7 mins. dead and myself 7 mins. 8 secs. Against these times, the best Jaguar time was Stirling's in 5 mins. 44 secs. ; Allard, Sydney Allard 6 mins. 6 secs. ; Aston Martin, Reg. Parnell 6 mins. 20 secs. ; H.R.G., Peter Clark 7 mins. 3 secs. ; Frazer-Nash, N. R. Culpan 5 mins. 49 secs. ; M.G., T. Lund 7 mins. 1 sec. ; and the lone Jowett Jupiter, driven by Tommy Wisdom, 7 mins. 10 secs.

I didn't know who had compiled the official bulletin of practice times, but whoever it was appeared to have a limited knowledge of the cars running in the race, for Tommy Wisdom's car was down as a Gowott Jupiter while Reg. Parnell and Lance Macklin were apparently driving Austin M's.

At last the car was ready again for the road but by the time I was back on the circuit it was after 1 o'clock and I only had time to do three slow laps, bedding the brakes down before all traffic was stopped between half past one and 2 p.m. As soon as they were open again for official practice I was off again although I now had to be very careful for everyone else on the course was going really fast while I was still trying to bed the brakes down gradually. Before long, I began to notice a noise towards the tail of the car and, stopping at the pits to investigate, I found that the offside rear wing had developed a crack which was rapidly running along parallel to the flange securing the wing to the body.

This was a fine thing for, from the point of view of the brakes I wanted to do as many miles as possible while, with a trouble of this sort I should obviously not be able to get far in any case. Official practice was already half over and there was not another chance of practice before the race so, brakes or no brakes, I decided to get going right away and to try to get in a respectable lap.

Conditions were much better than they had been on the previous evening and I now began to try hard to see what I could do. I had done about two laps and was just beginning to feel happier despite the awful clatter from the rear end when I discovered one of the Aston Martins on my tail. Letting him by, I found that it was George Abecassis and I was able to follow him for the best part of that lap.   I finally lost him though and continued by myself for another two or three laps, at the end of which I felt much happier.   I also felt fairly sure that I must have improved on my previous evening's practice time substantially and this was confirmed when I again pulled into the pits to consult my timekeepers, Jean and Anne, for although my lap times had started at around the seven-minute mark, I had now succeeded in pulling it down to 6 mins. 6 secs.

I felt very sure that I could still improve on this considerably for I had done only very few laps really at racing speeds, but the crack in the rear wing was now much worse and, coupled with this, the brakes had begun to bed down so that they were already requiring adjustment.

So although I should have liked much more practice, I had to remain content with things as they were.   I had improved my practice time but so, of course, had everyone else and the best times of each marque now stood as follows :

Jaguar (Stirling Moss), 5 mins. 28 secs., 81.39 m.p.h.
Aston Martin (L. Macklin), 5 mins. 50 secs., 76.28 m.p.h.
Healey (Ernie Wilkinson), 6 mins. dead, 74.16 m.p.h.
Frazer-Nash (N. R. Culpan), 5 mins. 44 secs., 77.61 m.p.h.
H.R.G. (Peter Clark), 6 mins. 38 secs., 67.08 m.p.h.
Jowett Jupiter (T. Wisdom), 6 mins. 28 secs., 68.80 m.p.h.
M.G. (Jacobs), 6 mins. 48 secs., 65.43 m.p.h. ;

while the lone Austin A.90, driven by J. C. Wilson which had done 7 mins. 12 secs. on the previous evening, now improved to 6 mins. 58 secs. or 63.87 m.p.h., my own time represented a speed of 72.94 m.p.h. and I hoped to improve on this appreciably in the race next day.

Apart from the brakes and the rear wing, everything else was absolutely all right with the car and we now got to work to cure what troubles we had.   I fully realized that we had not given the brakes nearly enough running and that we might well strike trouble in the race as a result of this and I had had further dire warnings from the technical " kings," but time was not on our side and had not been on our side since we had set foot in Ireland, so I set out to make the best of a bad job.

And a bad job it was as we realized when we awoke on the following morning to find leaden skies and a minor hurricane raging outside. However, we were in it up to the neck and we could only hope that things would improve before the race began at 2 p.m.   Having had breakfast, we made our way round to the garage to inspect the progress made on the car and found that repairs and adjustments were almost complete. Having checked and found that my presence was not required we decided to do some shopping which included food and drink for the unfortunate pit staff who looked like having a lean time of it in the pits up on the bleak hillside.

While the car had been garaged at Leslie Porter's, I had made the acquaintance of a young Irish enthusiast, David Michael who, although still at school, had little to learn about personalities in the motor-racing world and about the cars they drove.   David had looked me up as soon as we arrived and had kindly offered his help for the practice periods although, as he had to play in a match for his school on the Saturday, he was unable to come with us to the race.   At first, I confess, I was a little doubtful, because one receives a lot of offers of help from enthusiasts who later turn out to be liabilities rather than assets, but David's knowledge of motor racing was obviously so profound and his enthusiasm so great that I felt sure he would be a great help to us, quite apart from his very pleasant personality.   Almost immediately I was thankful that we had accepted his offer of help for, apart from his knowledge of the subject, he had, of course, a tremendous fund of local knowledge and was of the greatest assistance to us throughout our stay in Belfast.   Nothing at any time was too much trouble for him.   He always managed to keep on an even keel when things in our *équipe* were at their most difficult, and if any racing motorist visiting Ireland receives the offer of his help I would advise him most strongly to take it.   From such material do successful racing drivers emerge.

By now it was time for us to make our way up to the course with the car and all its impedimenta, for the roads were to be closed at 1 p.m. We left Belfast at twelve-thirty and had everything parked in and behind our pit by one fifteen. There was by now a full-scale tempest in operation and, for the life of me, I couldn't see how my poor pit staff would last out the three hours under the conditions prevailing although they, themselves, assured me that they were filled with quiet confidence. We were missing David's presence tremendously for these were the very conditions in which he seemed to thrive and had he been there I had no doubt that he would somehow have built us a tent or at least put forward some really constructive suggestion to make life much more tolerable for all concerned. However, there was little to be done and, fortunately, we had masses of rugs, coats, scarves, mackintoshes and other weather-defying equipment and we all agreed to stay in the Citroën until the last possible moment in the vain hope that conditions might improve. Meanwhile, assisted by Buckle who was now spare because " Buster " Baring had wisely decided that his Frazer-Nash had not had enough running and had therefore withdrawn from the race, we pressed on with the topping up of the Healey with fuel, oil and water.

The R.A.C. officials then sealed the tank for the last time, tyre pressures were checked by Dunlops, the spare being found to be below pressure and the tube being changed by them and the spare handed back to us at the pit in four minutes, and as the car was already warmed up from its run up from Belfast we were now set to go.

It was now ten to two. All engines had been stopped and I had a last word with poor Jean and Anne. I was worried about them both, for the rain was now falling steadily and was driving horizontally through the pits. I was particularly concerned about Jean, for she was only just beginning to shake off her cold and to stick it out in these pits for three hours was going to be about as bad a thing for her as one could imagine.

I told both girls that as I shouldn't be able to see any pit signals even if they gave them, the best thing they could do was to park themselves in the car behind the pits and to watch the race as best they could from there. If I came into the pits they would be on hand and as we were not allowed to carry out any work on the car using any tools other than those carried on the car, our pit presented a scene of desolation, the sole occupant being Maurice Buckle, Baring's capable and enthusiastic mechanic.

I had a last-minute disagreement with Jean as to what I should wear. I had previously agreed to wear a crash helmet and visor—had not even required any persuasion this time—but now, in addition to the numerous pullovers and sweaters I was wearing, I was instructed to wear a mackintosh as well. I protested and explained that not only could I not run properly at the start in a mackintosh but that I felt obstructed in the car by one. The argument was brief and I wore the mackintosh.

Now it was one fifty-five and, as at Silverstone, all the cars were lined up along the pits with the drivers opposite their respective machines. Incidentally, it had since transpired that at Silverstone, Cuthbert Harrison had made a spirited attempt to get into the wrong car, a strong argument arising in consequence, although I didn't think there was really any likelihood of this happening in my case because my Healey was the only red one of the lot, all the others being either green or blue.

At one minute to go, the conditions were as bad as ever and, as the final seconds ticked away, I watched the various preparations of those in the pits to combat the elements for the next three hours. If the drivers looked strange at Silverstone, they looked even stranger now and when I looked down the line and saw Lance Macklin waiting to drive his Aston Martin in a pixie hood I felt that I had witnessed everything that motor racing had to offer.

At last—five seconds to go, four, three, two—one—and down goes the flag. Again the mad scramble across the track—again the breathless silence having hurled oneself into the car and again the sudden realization that my engine was running before I, at least, had heard anyone else's. Into first gear—and away—and as I pull out, the entire line seems to pull out as well.

But again the start is a good one—there is no doubt about that, for there are no Healeys, or Frazer-Nashs ahead, only Allards, Jaguars and directly ahead, the three Aston Martin D.B. 2s. I just manage to scramble past the Austin A.90

before the narrow section which is good from my point of view
for, as the most " touring " car in the race, he is likely to hold
up very fast cars behind him quite appreciably.

Now we are really cracking along the straight at Rushyhill,
but as we approach the fast bends at the end of the straight
there is considerable caution among those at the head of the
procession and the stop lights of the three Aston Martins
directly ahead of me blink, it seems, hundreds of yards earlier
than they have done even in the worst weather in practice.

Leathemstown bridge is also treated with respect by all, but
the superior acceleration of the Aston Martins tells slightly
in the steep pull away afterwards.   Nevertheless, after the
breathtaking dive down to Cochranstown, I am again right
on the tail of the third one, driven I can now see by George
Abecassis, as we pull away from the corner.

I know very well that this state of affairs cannot and will
not last—that the field is gradually sorting itself out and that
we are all having a chance to assess carefully the fearful state
of the roads.   Because the process is taking slightly longer
than usual and the pace is, in consequence, considerably
slower, it would be a fatal mistake to try to pass even if it looks
possible to do so at this stage.

At Wheelers Corner the form is now taking shape, for the
Astons have drawn seventy or eighty yards ahead and I am
now trying really hard to keep up instead of, as at the start
of the lap, feeling I could get by.   We round the hairpin which
always gives one an impression of standing still after the fast
bends preceding and following it and, having successfully
negotiated the Quarry bends, we are passing the pits for the
first time.

Reading later from the official bulletin issued by the R.A.C.
I found that at the end of this lap I lay fourth in the class, our
respective averages for the first lap being : Reg. 65.59 m.p.h.,
Lance 63.14, George 62.82, all with Astons, of course, while I
followed at 62.09 m.p.h., with Ernie Wilkinson on the next
Healey, fifth at 61.23 m.p.h.   Leslie Johnson led the big boys
on his Jaguar at 69.34, followed by Stirling Moss, similarly
mounted, at 69.16 m.p.h., Allard with one of his own products
being third in this class at 65.92 m.p.h.   No one obviously

was prepared to risk getting into trouble on the first lap as these speeds showed. Incidentally, there had been no serious accidents in practice although Newton had been off the road in his Frazer-Nash and having repaired the fairly extensive damage had suffered mechanical trouble while testing the car on an airfield just before the start of the race. Nick Haines had also come unstuck in the Jaguar entered by him, but which was to have been driven by Tony Rolt, and although not badly hurt himself, it was found impossible to bring the car to the line at the start.

Although I didn't know it at the time, there was a smash on the second lap of the race which might well have had serious consequences, for my team mate, Walter Freed, who was just behind me at the time, came badly unstuck at Irelands Corner, the car apparently hitting the offside bank first, careering across the road and collecting a tree head on. The marshals at this spot must have been right on their toes for, granted the fact that the accident happened immediately behind me, there could only have been an interval of six and a half minutes at the outside before we were round again. At no time did I see any sign of the wrecked car and in that time they must somehow have dislodged the wreck from the tree and parked it somewhere well clear of the course—really smart work by all concerned. Freed was fortunately quite unhurt, apart from having broken his glasses which, having seen the car, seemed to me a miracle. Fairly early on lap two, I spied a dark green car in my mirror which obviously had the speed to pass, and pulling aside I found that it was Ernie Wilkinson. He passed, going great guns, and when we reached the pits at the end of that lap he was eight seconds ahead of me according to our timing.

To my great dismay, however, the brakes of the Healey were already showing signs of tiring. The symptoms were not the same as those I had had in practice, for there was now plenty of brake power, but the pedal was going farther and farther down to the boards which meant that, if we went on at this rate, there would be literally nothing left even by half distance. The state of affairs was exactly what I had been warned would happen if the brakes were not bedded down and progressively adjusted over a substantial mileage so I could place the blame on no one but myself although I felt that we had not really had the best of luck on this particular trip right from the outset. Nevertheless, there it was, the brakes were bedding down, and mighty quickly under these conditions, so I decided to give up trying to stay with Ernie and to brake earlier everywhere and use the gearbox wherever possible in an endeavour to keep going to the end somehow. One by one, the Frazer-Nashs of Culpan, Gerard and Crook came by, as I had expected, for we knew too well that due to their very light weight we couldn't hope to stick with them on the Healeys although at the start they had been slightly farther down the line due to their smaller capacity, but before long I found another Healey, this time Robin Richards, on my tail and again I had to let him pass.

Both Ernie Wilkinson and Robin were taking the bends at terrific speed and it was quite hopeless for me to try to tag along and still have any brakes later in the race ; but before long I found yet another Healey, this time the green car driven by Masters, on my tail. He passed me just before Jordans Cross, the car sounding very good indeed and on the run up to Wheelers Corner I noticed that it appeared to have rather more acceleration than either of the two Healeys that had passed me previously. Masters, however, was exercising much more caution on the bends than either Robin or Ernie, and as soon as he had gone by I tucked in behind him to watch points.

I found that, despite his superior acceleration I could gain a lot on him on the fast bends on the uphill stretch from Irelands Corner to the hairpin. He would pull away at the hairpin, I could gain on him again through the twisty bends before the pits whereupon he would pull right away on the long straight from the pits to Leathemstown Corner.

Over Leathemstown bridge I found that I was catching him again and by using the brakes fairly hard at Cochranstown I found that I was right on his tail once more half-way between Jordans Cross and Wheelers Corner. This went on for several laps until I noticed that already things were noticeably worse in the braking department and, bearing in mind the fact that we had not yet completed one hour's running out of three, I decided to save the brakes even more in my endeavours to finish the race.

Weather conditions had, for the past fifty minutes, been even worse but now it appeared as though it might be going to improve. Unfortunately the improvement was only temporary for by three-thirty they were as bad as ever. I was absolutely thankful that I had lost the argument over the mackintosh for although the rain had collected in a lake in my lap and had trickled down so that I sat in a sort of subterranean pool, I was comparatively dry from the waist up.

Even the pool in which I sat, and it really was a pool of some standing—for the water was pouring in a steady stream off the scuttle of the car—even this pool was mildly warm for, without using the brakes I was having to drive the old car to the maximum and the hard worked engine and gearbox were warming the cockpit nicely in consequence.

Strangely enough visibility did not seem to me to be too bad when one was alone, but in the company of other cars it was at times down almost to nil when the rain was at its height.

I was keeping a careful eye on both the time and the petrol gauge for we had checked on consumption and if it were wet we should just be able to run through the three hours without stopping for fuel by virtue of the reduced mileage we should cover under these conditions. If fine, we thought we should have to stop but, of course, although we couldn't possibly have had it wetter our calculations were now completely upset by the brakeless state in which we now found ourselves.

Not only was I having to drive the car much harder than I had intended to in order to put up even a reasonable performance, but in addition, I was having to use third and even second gears probably a hundred per cent. more than I had in practice in order to assist in pulling the car up. Towards the end of the race the situation from our point of view was so desperate that on two occasions I had to use first gear instead of second in order to get the car round the hairpin.

At the end of one and a half hours' running the needle of the fuel gauge showed the tank between half and three-quarters full, but I knew that in common with most other gauges it was prone to fall much more quickly from the half full to zero positions than from the full to half full points. Until later in the race I should not be able to learn much from it but I knew that when the car went on to reserve, I could then do only four more laps at the outside without running out of fuel.

Meanwhile, despite the awful conditions, or perhaps even because of them, the race was not by any means lacking in excitement. Allard, it was learned, had crashed into a field at Wheelers Corner, fortunately without hurting himself, and having investigated the position he was able to get the car out and back on to the road again, even getting it back to the pits where he was able to effect repairs which enabled him to get going again and to complete the course although at very much reduced speed. Culpan's Frazer-Nash had been reported slowing appreciably and it was later found that the cause here was that the unfortunate driver had had his visor damaged, presumably by a bird or some other foreign body, since he was not in the company of other cars at the time. The result was just the same, streams of water penetrating the visor, half blinding poor Culpan who did remarkably well to keep going at all under such conditions.

The only incident I had noticed was when I discovered one of the H.R.G. team stationary in the road right on the approach to the hairpin. As I passed, I could see that it was Peter Clark's car and to my great surprise it was still there when I came round again six and a half minutes or so later and I couldn't at the time imagine what malady had befallen it to make it immobile for so long. Looking back, although I am not absolutely sure, I think it was still there when I came round for the second time. At any rate I was vastly puzzled by it all and subsequently heard that its brakes had seized on which must have been a considerable source of worry to the marshals on the hairpin and, of course, even more so to Peter himself. Tommy Wisdom on the Jowett Jupiter had retired from the race with a blown cylinder head gasket while a number of people were reported to have had slides in the wet, some of them finishing by hitting the banks alongside the road.

Over the timed section after the pits Moss who was now leading the race easily was fastest with 120.5 m.p.h., Whitehead was next at 120 m.p.h., Johnson following closely at 119.3 m.p.h. Everything else seemed a good deal slower, Wilkinson managing 108.1 m.p.h., while Gerard and Murray on Frazer-Nashs recorded 106.8 m.p.h. and 104.9 m.p.h. respectively. A great deal depended on whether it was possible to get a clear run down the straight for, on a subsequent lap, Johnson was timed at only 116.5 m.p.h.

By 4 p.m. the conditions were absolutely indescribable, for in addition to the wind and driving rain the section of the course between Wheelers Corner and the hairpin was becoming shrouded in mist. On one lap it would be quite bad, then on the next it would have improved, while on the lap following it would move a few hundred yards down the road just to make it harder still. I found this complication, coupled with my brake troubles, almost the last straw that broke the camel's back and for a time I felt like packing the whole thing in. However, we had come a long way for the race and were now two-thirds through it and it seemed a pity to drop out at this stage, if we could possibly keep going, although we were, of course, nowhere in the running even for a class place. But the thing that decided me above all else to keep going was the marvellous enthusiasm and doggedness of the spectators and even more so the spirit among the marshals and observers all round the course. In all the races both on two wheels and on four that I have run I can never recall a race or a course where flag signals were of greater importance, and I can certainly say without fear of contradiction that I have never at any time seen those duties carried out more efficiently or under more unpleasant circumstances.

From the driver's point of view it was often impossible to know that there was a car behind one wishing to pass unless one received a flag signal, for at times the mirrors became coated in mud and water so that they were temporarily almost useless. Towards the latter part of the race in fact, the Aston Martins were using their sidelights and these showed up so well in my mirror when they came up behind that I at once followed suit and found passing quite a bit easier in consequence.

Just after four-thirty the car ran right out of fuel on the main supply just between Quarry Corner and the pits and this, too, presented another headache for I now knew that in the twenty-six minutes left before 5 p.m., when the race was due to finish, I should cover almost exactly four laps. Whether to make sure of completing the race by stopping on my last lap or whether to chance it and to keep going I couldn't decide. The car hadn't gone quite as far on main supply as it should have, according to the calculations we had made during practice, but this was obviously because I had had to use the gears so much more to assist in braking and this state of affairs would certainly be no better over the final four laps.

I thought and thought about it, and just couldn't decide. As we were not in the running we could lose little by coming in except that it would put us further still down the list of finishers.   On the other hand, if the car ran out of fuel between the hairpin and Quarry Corner, as it probably would on the last lap, it should, I felt, be able to coast the remainder of the way to the pits, most of this being downhill.   Another awful possibility occurred to me.   I had estimated that I should arrive at the finish almost spot on 5 o'clock.   Supposing I arrived seconds before to find no flag flying, I should then be faced with having to do yet another lap which was, I knew, quite impossible without a fuel stop.

Although I wasn't sure, I had a feeling that several of the other Healeys had stopped for fuel.   Mike Oliver in Guy's car, which was the only Healey which had been laying behind me for the greater part of the race, had passed me about six laps from the end.   Two laps later I had come upon him again going very slowly at Jordans Cross—obviously trying to nurse the car back to the pits.   That looked very like fuel shortage and later turned out to be just that.

Anyhow, I didn't decide until I was nearly beginning what I hoped and thought would be my last lap.   To tell the truth, I felt so disgusted with the prevailing conditions that, although I realized it was a chance, I decided to take it and to keep going.   If the thing ran out, nothing was lost ; if it didn't, so much the better.   I did, however, take one precaution in driving the car not quite so hard for the final lap.   In this way I may perhaps have saved the few drops of fuel necessary to take the car over the line, but I also ensured that it was fractionally after 5 o'clock rather than fractionally before it when I rounded Quarry Corner for the last time. Anyhow we made it and it was a great relief to see the chequered flag flying, although rather limply, as we arrived at the pits, followed closely by

Robin who had just failed to lap us and by Mike Oliver who, having passed us once, had then had to stop for fuel and had just failed to catch up and pass for the second time.

The scene at the pits was quite chaotic for the gale which was now certainly worse than ever, had blown down most of the refreshment tents, the rain was falling as never before and as, one by one, the storm-battered cars and drivers arrived the confusion and shouting increased. Needless to say, my wonderful wife was waiting, soaked to the skin, to welcome me, for all our efforts to combat the elements whether in the car or in the pits had been as naught.

We packed up our stuff at high speed in an endeavour to get back to Belfast and hot baths before the car parks began to empty and the roads became blocked. Poor Walter Freed, who was without transport as a result of his crash, came back with me in the Healey while his assistant accompanied Jean and Anne in the Citroën. We were only partly successful in our manœuvre to get away before the traffic got out of hand and by the time we had got back to the hairpin the roads at that point were crammed.

A one-way traffic system had been put into operation which, although it obviously fulfilled its purpose, which was to keep the traffic moving, seemed likely to take us a long way round and was unpopular with us in consequence.

The police officers in charge were adamant, however, but when they caught sight of Freed and me in the Healey they appeared so shaken that they let us through on the direct road without a murmur.

As a result, we were separated from the other section of the party in the Citroën and when we arrived at Leslie Porter's there was no transport to take us back to the hotel. As I never carry anything in my pockets when racing I had no money for a taxi and as we couldn't spot one anyway, we decided to walk. We were joined almost immediately by David, hotfoot from his match in the course of which he had been kicked in the face, although this was in no way damping his enthusiasm and his desire to hear first hand all about the race.

I

As we tramped through the main streets of Belfast *en route* for the Grand Central Hotel, I couldn't help thinking what an odd trio we must look and was not in the least surprised to find all and sundry staring at us.   David, very tall and wearing his school cap with his face very battered, Walter, still wearing what remained of his spectacles after his crash in the early part of the race and finally myself, soaked to the skin, still wearing the mackintosh in which I had driven.   Trousers tucked into my socks and face as black as a sweep's.   It has always been a source of wonderment to me that we were not taken in charge during the course of that walk, for if ever three citizens shouted " physical violence," we did, by virtue of our appearance.   Arriving back at the hotel we found that the other half of the party had just beaten us to it although, as far as we could see, no one else had yet arrived back from the race.

Having regaled ourselves with hot baths and tea upstairs in our room, we compared notes of our respective reactions during the three hours of the race.   The girls had stuck it out in the pits for the best part of an hour after all, but finding it quite impossible to maintain any sort of lasting protection against the elements, they had at last retired to the warmth of the Citroën parked behind the pits.   They hadn't really seen any of the race because it is practically impossible to follow actual race progress from that point unless one is actually in the pits themselves.   Despite this, they had had a constant stream of rain-sodden visitors from the pits to keep them in touch with the state of progress.   The heroes of the day were the Jaguar team who had put up by far the best performances, both outright and on handicap, the complete list of finishers on formula being as follows :—

	Miles	m.p.h.	Percentage of Handicap
1. S. Moss, 3,442-c.c. Jaguar ...	225.45	75.15	97.47
2. P. N. Whitehead, 3,442-c.c. Jaguar	222.392	74.13	96.15
3. F. R. Gerard, 1,971-c.c. Frazer-Nash	219.18	71.92	96.02

4.	R. Parnell, 2,580-c.c. Aston Martin	200.325	72.72	95.93
5.	G. Abecassis, 2,580-c.c. Aston Martin	199.565	72.38	95.49
6.	N. R. Culpan, 1,971-c.c. Frazer-Nash	213.452	71.15	94.99
7.	L. G. Johnson, 3,442-c.c. Jaguar	219.18	73.06	94.76
8.	L. Macklin, 2,580-c.c. Aston Martin	215.354	71.78	94.69
9.	E. J. Wilkinson, 2,443-c.c. Healey	211.791	70.59	93.37
10.	T. A. D. Crook, 1,971-c.c. Frazer-Nash	207.739	69.25	92.46
11.	Robin Richards, 2,443-c.c. Healey	206.624	68.87	91.10
12.	C. H. Masters, 2,443-c.c. Healey	206.390	68.79	90.99
13.	D. H. Murray, 1,971-c.c. Frazer-Nash	203.23	67.74	90.44
14.	C. Mortimer, 2,443-c.c. Healey	199.451	66.48	87.93
15.	M. Oliver, 2,443-c.c. Healey ...	199.284	66.43	87.87
16.	R. W. Jacobs, 1,250-c.c. M.G., TD.	189.892	63.29	87.54
17.	G. Warburton, 4,375-c.c. Allard	200.934	66.97	85.31
18.	K. Watkins, 4,375-c.c. Allard	199.565	66.52	84.73
19.	G. E. Phillip, 1,250-c.c. M.G., TD.	182.621	60.87	84.19
20.	E. W. K. Lund, 1,250-c.c. M.G., TD.	180.990	60.33	83.44
21.	John Buncombe, 1,496-c.c. H.R.G.	179.342	59.78	80.67
22.	J. J. Flynn, 1,250-c.c. M.G., TC.	171.068	57.02	78.86
23.	" T. Flack," 1,250-c.c. M.G., TD.	170.771	56.92	78.73
24.	A. P. Hitching, 1,496-c.c. H.R.G.	174.816	58.27	78.64
25.	W. B. Groves, 1,250-c.c. M.G., TC.	167.759	55.92	77.34
26.	M. Healsett, 1,250-c.c. M.G., TC.	167.238	55.74	77.10
27.	S. H. Allard, 4,375-c.c. Allard	162.881	54.29	69.16

There was no doubt about it, that the Jaguars thoroughly deserved their win and that their drivers had really excelled themselves. Everyone in the race had had their problems, the Jaguars main headache probably being the difficulty of passing slower cars, while the Aston Martin drivers in their saloons were almost entirely dependent on the durability and power of their screen wipers.

The day must have been a little disappointing for the Frazer-Nashs and for that matter for the M.G.s and Allards. The drivers of the H.R.G.s were outclassed and the same could perhaps be said of our own cars. But, to me, the satisfaction of having got to the finish of such a " Classic " Classic outweighed absolutely everything, for it can truthfully be said that there had never so far been one to compare with this for weather conditions. To quote just one report, that of the *Sporting Life* :

" The 1950 R.A.C. Tourist Trophy Race, revived in Northern Ireland last Saturday after a lapse of twelve years, and run over the new $7\frac{1}{4}$-mile Dundrod Circuit, Co. Antrim, will ever be remembered by drivers and spectators alike as one run under the worst conditions imaginable ; so bad, indeed, that it is safe to say that no race in history has been run in such appalling circumstances. The wind was of hurricane force, the rain from start to finish was torrential, and the visibility poor. Under these conditions it was amazing that speeds were so high and that the race was devoid of personal injury to the participants."

We had planned to put the car on a cargo boat leaving Belfast on Sunday at midday, while we ourselves were flying back to Liverpool on Sunday afternoon and were hoping to collect the cars there in the evening. We awoke on Sunday morning to find everything much as before although the rain had abated slightly by now. I walked round to the garage after breakfast, collected the Healey, took it down to the docks, came back for the Citroën and delivered that also. I saw the mate of the cargo boat who said that we should definitely stand no chance of collecting the cars that night so I went back to the hotel to report.

We were due to report at the Air Terminal in Belfast at three-fifteen, but on arrival there, we found the place packed out and no little uncertainty about when our plane would actually leave.   This was quite understandable in view of everything, so we went back again to the hotel where we were joined by Mike Oliver for tea.   Mike was also trying to make his way home by air and we ultimately beat him to it, leaving Belfast about five-thirty, having another wait at the airport, and finally arriving at the Adelphi Hotel in Liverpool in time for dinner.   There we found Robin Richards who had left on the passenger boat the previous evening and who, in company with many other unfortunates, had just got in after a crossing which absolutely defied description.   After an early night, for we had had a late one after the race, we were down at the docks in good time to find that the car had already been unloaded and that the Citroën was in the process of unloading as we arrived.   We grabbed both cars gratefully and made our way home, Jean and Anne taking over the Healey, while I followed with the goods and chattels.

The faithful old Healey had once again finished without discredit at any rate.   Everything had stayed put, the only things requiring adjustment being the brakes and one rear shock absorber and once these had been done the car was ready for the last meeting of the season at Goodwood on September 30th.

Much to my disappointment, I found that I was likely to be unable to drive the car this time for, although I knew I could get down to Goodwood for the race, I was not certain about practising on the Friday due to certain business commitments which, unfortunately, I couldn't alter.   I wanted the car to run and as Jean couldn't drive it either, ladies not being eligible to compete at the Goodwood main meetings, I asked George Abecassis if he would deputize for me and was very pleased when he agreed to do so.

The car was running in one short handicap only and, at the last moment, I was able to get away for Friday afternoon and met George at Goodwood, having rushed there straight from the office in the Minor.   George had motored himself down in the Healey in order to have a bit of driving in the car before taking it out on the circuit and as his co-director John Heath was unavoidably absent for the day, I gladly agreed to do some work with the stop watch for the H.W.M. team which consisted of two cars, each of which was being driven by two drivers at various stages of the meeting.

The first car, number 15, was to have been driven by George and John, but in John's absence, Duncan Hamilton was taking his place while the second, number 16, was being shared by Stirling Moss and Tony Rolt, and it was agreed that the Healey should practise after the H.W.M.s had completed their sessions.

George had some steady running to do on his car before he began to practise seriously and he and Stirling went out together immediately the circuit was open for their section of the entries. Clocking both cars every lap meant operating four stop watches at one time and for the next two hours I found I was kept really busy and had to concentrate quite hard in order not to miss a lap time or make a mistake which might lead the team up the garden in any way.

Stirling went out and began to go fast right away, doing only five laps, his times being 1.47, 1.43, 1.42, 1.41 and 1.41, fantastically good for an unblown 2-litre car on a course of this nature. George, having completed his running in on the other car, replied with 1.45, 1.44, 1.45, 1.44, 1.45, 1.44, 1.43 and 1.43, also most creditable and causing our hopes to run high for the morrow. Reg. Parnell was out on the circuit at the same time with the B.R.M. which was endeavouring to regain some prestige after its ignominious failure at Silverstone and although I didn't get it on the watch myself, being too fully occupied at the time, I heard people quoting its time as 1 min. 39 secs. odd, and being vastly impressed thereby.

Although I realized that Reg. must, of necessity, be driving with some care I couldn't myself see that this was an awfully impressive figure when compared with Stirling's laps of 1.41, although in common with everyone else I was awaiting with the keenest anticipation the B.R.M's showing in the Woodcote Cup and Goodwood Trophy races next day.

As the car that George had driven now required some minor adjustments it was agreed that both Duncan and Tony should practise on the other car and Duncan then went out, recording 1.50, 1.47, 1.44, 1.45, 1.42, 1.42 and 1.45, being baulked by a a slower car at Woodcote Corner on his final lap. Tony was busy with his Alfa at this time so George then took over the

Healey, doing four consecutive laps of 1.59, then 1.56 and four laps of 1.55.   He came in to alter the tyre pressures slightly and continued with 1.55, 1.54, 1.54 and 1.53, his final lap being fractionally the best any of us had done with the car on this circuit.

By now, the afternoon was nearly over and Tony, having finished his practice laps with the Alfa, took the H.W.M. out for only four laps, the best of which was 1.45.   He had never driven the car before and was tremendously impressed with it as was everyone who had been fortunate enough to have driven these wonderful little cars.

Thus finished our day's practice, and we now had only one more day's racing to complete our 1950 season's racing.   We hoped that it would be fine after our visit to Ireland, but one look at the weather on Saturday morning gave us the answer. It would be true to say that conditions were no worse than they had been for the T.T., although they really seemed very little better.

Arriving in the paddock at Goodwood on Saturday morning took us right back to the opening meeting of the season when, once again, conditions had been just like these.   But on this occasion it was poor George and not I who had to brave the elements.   In Ireland he had remained warm and dry inside the lovely Aston Martin D.B.2 coupé.   Now he faced the prospect of no less than three wet drives in one afternoon, for the H.W.M. was to run in a handicap as well as in the Goodwood Trophy race.

The first race of major interest was the third of the day, the Woodcote Cup, in which the B.R.M. was running, its challengers being, amongst others, de Graffenried, Bira and David Hampshire on 4CLT Maseratis, Poore on his big 3.8 Alfa and Bob Gerard, Brian Shawe Taylor and Peter Whitehead on E.R.A.s.   At the fall of the flag, the B.R.M. was left slightly, possibly because Reg. was making sure of avoiding a repetition of the Silverstone fiasco and as the cars disappeared from view it was de Graffenried's red Maserati that led the pack.

The rain was teeming down and we had parked the Citroën in the paddock facing the Lavant straight and in a very few seconds we could hear the cars rounding the gradual bend into the straight and accelerating away.   Almost immediately we could see them.   Yes—a red car still led but with the light green B.R.M. right on its tail and as we watched, the B.R.M. appeared to gather itself together absolutely hurtling past the Maserati, giving it the impression of standing still.   The crowd went mad.   It was exactly what they had wanted to see—in many cases had contributed their hard earned pennies to see, and were they pleased !

On the next lap, Reg. had increased his lead even more, but on the third, realizing he had the race in his pocket, he was content to maintain his position, completing his final two laps with great restraint and winning comfortably.   Although it had to be agreed that the opposition was not all that strong, the B.R.M. had, in that one short race, shown the ray of hope for which everyone had waited.

In race five, George was driving the H.W.M. from the 25-sec. mark, the limit man being G. A. Ruddock's H.R.G. receiving 1 min. 20 secs. while in the absence of Bira and Ashmore, Peter Whitehead was virtual scratch man, having been allowed 10 secs. start from Bira in five laps.   The race looked a good thing for George who was giving Duncan Hamilton's six-cylinder Maserati 10 secs. also.

This was, of course, the car that had finished behind " Buster " Baring's H.W.M. when I had driven it at Jersey and I felt sure that, on this occasion the race lay between Duncan and George.   At the end of the first lap, George had gained over three seconds on Duncan and on lap two had gained another three and, if all went well, would obviously catch him some time early on in the last lap.   Unfortunately, however, at the end of his third lap the car spun round in the rain at Woodcote, enabling Duncan to continue and win with comparative ease.

Next, after another handicap, came race number seven in which the Healey was to run.   I had been warming the car up while George was driving the H.W.M. and as the sixth race was being run off we studied the programme to try and assess our chance, if any, on handicap.   We were down in the programme to start from the 25-second mark, but there were a number of non-starters which included all those due to give us start so that, in the end, we started from virtual scratch.

I had been able to get the times of most runners in the race during the practice period on the previous day and we now concluded that, unless anything unforeseen occurred, we could hope to achieve third place. The limit man was Wells' M.G. driven by Donald McLure and we established that if we repeated our lap speed of 76.5 m.p.h., represented by the time of 1 min. 53 secs., which we had done in practice, McLure would have to manage about 2 mins. 5 secs. or 69 m.p.h. in order to dead-heat with us. He had not lapped at anywhere near this speed in practice on any lap on which I had got him and with the exception of two cars, no one else has, according to my timing, been ahead of us on handicap.

The two cars with which I knew we couldn't cope were Lycett's huge 8-litre Bentley, capably driven by Leslie Johnson, and Shillito's Formula 2 unblown 2-litre Riley. We had to give both these cars six seconds' start which, manifestly, we couldn't afford to do for the Bentley had lapped at 1 min. 50 secs. on the previous day while the Riley was faster still having lapped, according to my timing, at between one forty-five and one forty-six at a previous meeting.

Again, something appeared to have gone slightly haywire with the handicapping here for, although the Bentley had not raced at Goodwood before to my knowledge and was therefore an unknown quantity from the handicappers' point of view, there must have been a stack of information regarding Shillito's car which had in the past been a consistent performer on this circuit.

Even as compared with the Bentley, the position was rather grotesque for a small fortune was said to have been spent on this monster by its owner, Forrest Lycett, who had quoted some fantastic figures regarding its performance, while our poor old Healey which was still running on Pool petrol was now concluding a season's racing without having had so much as a decoke.

Nevertheless, we could only do our best and we came to the line hoping that there were no other dark horses on whom we had failed to place our finger in practice. The start of the race was rather chaotic because having arrived on the line before anyone else, the limit M.G., driven by McLure, stopped its engine just as the flag was raised and despite the united efforts of its attendants and harassed driver, obstinately refused to start again.   The starter, with flag raised, was in a quandary, for McLure had stopped his engine before the fall of the flag and so the race had obviously not actually started, nor had the timekeepers in their box started their watches.   At long last, the chaos sorted itself out and one by one the runners were despatched.

At the end of the first lap I checked the gap between Leslie Johnson and our car and found that it had increased although we appeared to be coping satisfactorily with everyone else except Shillito.   On lap two the same state of affairs existed. Rather to my surprise, Leslie Johnson had led Shillito at the end of the first lap, but the order had then been reversed and the gap was widening rapidly between the two cars at the end of lap three.

Half-way through the fourth lap, George on the Healey moved up into fourth place having passed Guy Gale who had taken over Lyons' Connaught.   From then on, the order never changed and thus we finished our 1950 racing season with yet another place, but still having failed to score an outright win.

There was still one more highlight, however, for there was now the Goodwood Trophy to round off the day and in this race, of course, the B.R.M. was again running, this time over twelve laps of the 2.4-mile circuit.   The opposition was the same as in the Woodcote Cup and after its win in that race everyone waited eagerly to see the result of this race.   Only one H.W.M. was running on this occasion, George's car having developed trouble earlier in the afternoon making Stirling the sole representative of the marque.

At the fall of the flag, the events of the Woodcote Cup were repeated almost to the letter and at the end of the first lap the B.R.M. was again comfortably in the lead except that this time it was Bira and not de Graffenried who was doing the pressing. At the conclusion of the third lap it was obvious that Bira was by no means content to sit and watch Reg. score a walk-over and he began to put up a most spirited opposition, leaving his braking on the wet track to the last possible moment, saving the last fraction of a second on each bend and pushing the red Maserati to the maximum. Reg., on the other hand, wisely exercised the greatest caution on the bends and was content to rely on the really terrific acceleration of the B.R.M. to make up his leeway.

The result was, of course, the same as in the previous race. Reg., really driving with his head, under the most unenviable conditions possible, won the race his own way, sending some thousands of rain-sodden enthusiasts home happy in the knowledge that the car really could go after all.

Now it was time for us to pack up all our kit again for the last time of the season and as we did so, we reflected on the tremendous fun we had had from the car at, comparatively speaking, little cost. Perversely, the sun broke through just as the last race finished, although we had by now got so used to wet meetings that we had almost come to regard them as part of the set up.

Having brought the car down, George was going to take it back so, to round off the day and the 1950 season as well, we all met up again at the Talbot Hotel at Ripley. There, after another excellent dinner, we managed to find a dark corner in the bar where, until closing time, we sat listening to each fresh arrival from Goodwood describing the events of the day. As the evening wore on, the descriptions became more and more graphic until, in the end, we almost wished that we hadn't been there to see for ourselves !

Returning once more to the question of expense, it will be recalled that our first six months' running with the car had cost us just over £72, while our returns had amounted to between £35 and £36. On looking at the situation at the conclusion of the season, the accounts work out approximately as follows :

	£	s.	d.
Expenses from January 1st to June 30th, 1950 (already itemized)	72	3	0
Entry fees, July 1st to September 30th	27	14	6
Fuel and oil, July 1st to September 30th (Silverstone Production Car Race and R.A.C. Tourist Trophy included) 105 gallons	16	3	9

	£	s.	d.
Maintenance and work done other than by ourselves	24	10	0
Tyres	37	18	0
Silverstone Production Car Race : hotels and incidentals	25	0	0
Insurance of the car while running in the T.T. and at the final Goodwood Meeting, September 30th ...	22	10	0
Tourist Trophy, including fares and freight for three persons and two cars, hotel and garage bills ...	105	15	4
Jersey International Road Race, including fares for three persons and freight of H.W.M. and lorry, hotel and garage bills	100	0	0

			£	s.	d.
TOTAL			£431	14	7
Less bonus and prize money :					
January 1st to June 30th	£35	13	0		
July 1st to September 30th ...	105	0	0		
			140	13	0
TOTAL			£291	1	7

So when all was said and done, our season's racing had cost us just under £300.

Digging into the accounts, certain interesting points come to light, the main one being that although motor racing is never cheap, it can be comparatively cheap provided one restricts one's activities to events that don't necessitate crossing water. It has seemed from the rough figures we have kept that it is not so much the size of event as its location, which has a direct bearing on the question of expense.

All our day meetings, practically without exception, cost us only a few shillings more than they would had we taken the car or any saloon of comparable size and gone to spectate instead of compete. From a running point of view the car has cost us no more than an ordinary touring car would have done over the same mileage. What we were aiming for when we set out at the start of the season was plenty of racing in a car sufficiently fast to be interesting to drive and at the minimum possible cost.

As we saw it, speed is always expensive. The faster your car the more expensive it will be to run and maintain, and the faster it is the more interest and glamour surrounds it. If you are in a position to acquire the car embodying the most speed and therefore the most interest and glamour you pick Formula 1 and make out a cheque somewhere in the region of £5,000 for your car and another one for about half that amount to run it during its first season. If you still want Formula 1 but can't produce this money you lay out around £1,500 for your car with about half that figure for your first season's running expenses knowing that, if you are lucky, you will get as much running as your friend with his £5,000 motor-car, but that, while he can hope to get some of this cash back in prize money and bonus, yours will almost certainly all go down the drain.

The next step down the ladder is Formula 2 and here the choices are much more attractive. It would probably be true to say that you could spend £1,000 and could become the owner of a potential winner of some Formula 2 races run over a comparatively short distance. For between double and treble that figure you could probably own the best in that class although I think it would be true to say that, here again you would have to allow yourself, for running expenses, a sum considerably in excess of that which you would need to do a season's racing on the best sports car you could buy.

Your next choice, then, lies between a sports car and a Formula 3 machine, and both fields have so many supporters that I shouldn't really like to be called upon to draw a comparison between the two. We bought a sports car, largely because we wanted a car that we could use every day on the road besides being able to race. We knew, or hoped we knew, just what we could afford to outlay to buy the car although we were a bit in the dark as to how much to set aside in order to race it. We bought what we hoped and thought would be the fastest and most reliable car that we could for the money, and at the end of the season we felt satisfied that we had had value for our money.

We ran the car whenever and wherever we could and it only once really let us down unavoidably. We neither of us had a great deal of time to spend on it although we realized that properly maintained it must be, and if we couldn't do the work on it ourselves, someone else must. On the score of expense, we certainly didn't always do it the cheapest way. We always

stayed at the best hotels when we went away, some of their
charges shaking us to the core. We realized that with two of
us driving, the car was doing a much bigger mileage in practice
than it would with only one driver although the total number
of miles done in races probably amounted to no more than if
there had been one driver for, at all the Club Meetings, the
car ran in every available race driven by one or the other of us.

It is interesting to note that either one of the two races, the
T.T. with the Healey or the Jersey Race with the H.W.M.,
cost more than all the rest of our small races put together.
While we enjoyed them both tremendously, particularly the
Jersey Race, I don't really think they were worth the extra cost,
that is if the cost means anything, as it certainly did to us.
The B.R.D.C. Production Car Race at the *Daily Express*
Silverstone Meeting was, in my opinion, far better value,
even if the accounts hadn't come near to balancing, as they
very nearly did. But, looking back, I honestly think that we
got far more enjoyment and pleasure from the Club Meetings
even if one sets aside all costs, but if you take the question of
expense into consideration, I don't really think there is any
comparison.

Again, getting back to the expense angle, let's see whether
the job could have been done more cheaply by choosing
another sort of mount. Whichever way you look at it, I can't
see how it could be done unless you go in for a much slower
car, in which case I do think that a lot of the fun and excitement
is lost. There are, I know, some very fast vintage cars (I know
I'm treading on dangerous ground here !), but having talked
to some of the owners they seem as though they can be pretty
expensive to maintain if it is desired to keep them in winning
form, and in any case I think it must be agreed that with a
machine of this description you haven't nearly the scope that
you've got with a production car.

There is another way of cutting down expense and one which
I think is probably the best bet of all and that is by spending
double the money and sharing the product between two of you.
I don't think that anyone would maintain that our car was a
potential winner in many of the major events in which we ran
it, but by outlaying the same amount of capital you could, I
should have said, be half owner of a potential winner in some

of them at any rate although the snag here is that you do want to know your partner well and, to my mind, you must have the thing tied up by a firm agreement.

Going another rung down the ladder, you could, of course, become part owner in a car in the price range of ours and if I had to cut expense down even more I think that this is what I should be tempted to do. I haven't the slightest doubt that our car can be made to go very much faster than it has to date, although some money—not a lot—would have to be outlaid in order to make it do so.

We feel that although we should like to run next season we don't want to do exactly the same thing again. If we are going to continue with this car, we must make it go appreciably faster. We think we know just how much money we'll have to spend and also how much faster the car can be made to go, although we realize the ease with which calculations of this sort can go astray.

On the other hand, we have considered some of the alternatives already mentioned. We feel that our car has as good a reputation as most others of the breed and that, if we decide to, we could make a reasonably good sale and we know that, whatever course we take, we must decide by the end of the year at the latest so as to leave time properly to prepare whatever car we do decide to run next year.

These are, I suppose, the problems that every driver faces at the end of the season however deep or shallow his pocket may be. One of the snags of racing, from the driver's point of view, is the speed with which new and improved designs are doled out and it is easy even to start the season with the best and to be way down the list six months later. Probably the best antidote to this evil is in being able to drive slightly better than the next man and also to know your car slightly better, the answer in this case being largely found in constant practice. It is amazing what some drivers have achieved in the past when driving much slower cars than their rivals, purely by knowing just exactly what they could and could not do with their own car. A remarkable example of this was to be found in Prince Bira who, before the war, collected race after race against the most formidable opposition on sheer driving ability, organization and knowledge of his car.

Lastly, I should like to claim the reader's indulgence for any inaccuracies or misdescriptions of which I may have been guilty when describing the various events in which my wife and I have taken part. I have tried throughout to get my facts as accurate as possible, but I don't claim to be a journalist in the professional sense. Our object from first to last has been to present to those interested the problems besetting the amateur who is keen to enjoy some motor racing and if I have at any time trodden on anyone's toes I am extremely sorry.

If, also, we have, in writing this book, been of any assistance at all in starting lines of thought in the minds of those interested, then we have fulfilled our object and if, at any time we can help anyone who is keen to race, no matter on how small a scale, it will give us both the greatest possible pleasure.